MW01681228

REVOLUTION BETRAYED

America Rebuilt the System the Founders Fought a War to Secede From

Michael Boldin

TENTH Amendment CENTER

Contents

Chapter 1

THE REAL REVOLUTION

"*An elective despotism is not the government we fought for.*"

Thomas Jefferson warned about the dangers of unchecked power - even in a system where the people get to choose their leaders.

Yet an "elective despotism" is just what we ended up with.

Most people would immediately reject that claim, but the evidence is overwhelming. Because the system we live under today is virtually the same - in practice - as the British system the founders and old revolutionaries fought a long, bloody war to secede from.

The only practical difference comes down to elections every few years. But, as Thomas Paine warned, simply choosing who wields power doesn't actually make you free.

"It is not because a part of the government is elective, that makes it less a despotism, if the persons so elected possess afterwards, as a parliament, unlimited powers. Election, in this case, becomes

separated from representation, and the candidates are candidates for despotism."

This all comes down to a widespread misunderstanding of what the American Revolution was actually about.

NOT THE WAR

Most of us are taught that the American Revolution **was** the War for Independence. Writing to Thomas Jefferson, John Adams vehemently rejected that as not just wrong, but missing the forest for the trees.

"What do We mean by the Revolution? The War? That was no part of the Revolution. It was only an Effect and Consequence of it."

By the early part of the 19th Century, some were already making the mistake of conflating the War with the Revolution that preceded it. Adams recognized this in one of a series of letters to his long-time friend and ardent supporter, Rev. Jedidiah Morse.

"An History of military Operations from April 19th. 1775 to the 3d of September 1783 is not an History of the American Revolution."

If the war wasn't the revolution, what was? As Adams described it to Jefferson, it happened somewhere no army ever marched.

"The Revolution was in the Minds of the People, and this was effected, from 1760 to 1775, in the course of fifteen Years before a drop of blood was drawn at Lexington."

THE AMERICAN MIND

This "real American Revolution" formed the basis of what the Declaration of Independence was built on. Which, as Thomas Jefferson explained, wasn't about inventing something new at all.

"This was the object of the Declaration of Independence: not to find out new principles, or new arguments, never before thought of, not merely to say things which had never been said before; but to place before mankind the common sense of the subject."

It was, as he put it, something far more powerful than philosophy: a statement of what Americans already understood, believed, and lived.

"It was intended to be an expression of the American mind, and to give to that expression the proper tone and spirit called for by the occasion."

Like Jefferson and the Declaration, Adams described this "real American Revolution" as a once-in-a-lifetime, monumental transformation. It wasn't just about what the people did, but what they learned - and who they became.

"I mean a compleat Revolution in the Minds of the People. A total Change of the Opinions and Affections of The People, and a full Confidence in the practicability of a Union of the Colonies. All this was done and the Principles all established and the System matured before the year 1775. The War and the Peace followed of Course."

While the Declaration condensed fifteen years of this historic paradigm shift into one timeless document, Adams wrote that it wasn't abstract theory cooked up in private. It was a public revolution - printed and debated across thirteen colonies in real time.

"The Records of thirteen Legislatures, the Pamphlets, Newspapers in all the Colonies ought be consulted, during that Period, to ascertain the Steps by which the public opinion was enlightened and informed concerning the Authority of Parliament over the Colonies."

Jefferson agreed, noting the principles expressed in the Declaration itself could be traced directly to those public debates and the foundational texts that built them

"All it's authority rests then on the harmonising sentiments of the day, whether expressed, in conversns in letters, printed essays or in the elementary books of public right, as Aristotle, Cicero, Locke, Sidney Etc."

THIRTEEN CLOCKS

But as Adams noted in a letter to Hezekiah Niles, agreeing on principles was one thing. Getting thirteen vastly different colonies - with different cultural, political, economic and religious views - to act on those principles together? That was something else entirely.

"The Colonies had grown up under Constitutions of Government, So different, there was so great a Variety of Religions, they were composed of So many different Nations, their Customs, Manners and Habits had So little resemblance, and their Intercourse had been so rare and their Knowledge of each other So imperfect, that to unite them in the Same Principles in Theory and the Same System of Action was certainly a very difficult Enterprize."

Despite those incredibly difficult odds, the Revolution - and the independence that followed - still succeeded, something Adams considered to be without precedent in human history.

"The compleat Accomplishment of it, in So Short a time and by Such Simple means, was perhaps a Singular Example in the History of Mankind. Thirteen Clocks were made to Strike together; a perfection of Mechanism which no Artist had ever before effected."

What drove those separate clocks to strike at the exact same moment wasn't mere political calculation or shared economic interest. It ran, as Adams put it, far deeper.

"The Revolution was in the Minds and Hearts of the People. A Change in their Religious Sentiments of their Duties and Obligations."

That change had multiple pillars.

A new understanding of where power comes from and who holds it. Who decides when that power is unauthorized, and therefore not obligatory on the people. A clear-eyed recognition of when power is abused as a system, and the conviction that when such a danger strikes, resistance isn't just a right - it's a duty.

"This radical Change in the Principles, Opinions Sentiments and Affection of the People, was the real American Revolution."

But a radical change in the minds of the people doesn't spring out of nothing. It has to be built on something. A foundation - a set of principles already accepted, already understood, and already in the air.

Chapter 2

NATURAL RIGHTS

Rights aren't gifts from government. They don't come from documents, either.

They are created within us as a gift - and they exist as rights whether government agrees or not.

That truth was already woven into America's DNA long before independence was won, or even declared. So the Second Continental Congress could state in the Declaration of Independence what the people already understood.

"We hold these truths to be self-evident, that all men are created equal, that they are endowed by their Creator with certain unalienable Rights, that among these are Life, Liberty and the pursuit of Happiness."

READING LIST

As we've already seen, Thomas Jefferson insisted that the Declaration didn't cover new ground - it was built on "*the harmonising sentiments of the day.*"

Those sentiments were drawn directly from the letters, public essays, and foundational works of the era: "*Aristotle, Cicero, Locke, Sidney Etc.*"

In early 1775, a young Alexander Hamilton also shared a reading list of the great natural rights philosophers who influenced the American Revolution.

"Apply yourself, without delay, to the study of the law of nature. I would recommend to your perusal, Grotius. Puffendorf, Locke, Montesquieu, and Burlemaqui. I might mention other excellent writers on this subject; but if you attend, diligently, to these, you will not require any others."

THE SOURCE

As you read through the essays of the American Revolution, a common thread appears: Rights are not gifts from government - or, as John Dickinson put it, they never were.

"Kings or parliaments could not give the rights essential to happiness."

They don't come from documents - not a constitution, not even a bill of rights.

"They are not annexed to us by parchments and seals. They are created in us by the decrees of Providence, which establish the laws of our nature."

Those laws, as James Otis, Jr. explained, are immutable.

"The law of nature, was not of man's making, nor is it in his power to mend it, or alter its course. He can only perform and keep, or disobey and break it."

Even England's greatest legal mind of the time, William Blackstone, held that they outrank everything: Every government, legislature, court and manmade law on earth.

"This law of nature, being coeval with mankind and dictated by God himself, is of course superior in obligation to any other-It is binding over all the globe in all countries, and at all times; no human laws are of any validity, if contrary to this: and such of them as are valid derive all their force, and all their authority, mediately or immediately, from this original."

This natural law, as Hamilton continued, is the foundation of all natural rights.

"Upon this law, depend the natural rights of mankind, the supreme being gave existence to man, together with the means of preserving and beatifying that existence."

What are those natural rights?

Samuel Adams had the answer. But notice his framing: this wasn't an exhaustive list. It was only the starting point.

"Among the natural rights of the Colonists are these: First, a right to life; Secondly, to liberty; Thirdly, to property; together with the right to support and defend them in the best manner they can."

For Adams, the existence of these rights was obvious - and directly tied to the right of self-defense and the duty of self-preservation.

"These are evident branches of, rather than deductions from, the duty of self-preservation, commonly called the first law of nature."

THE FOUNDATION

The American Revolutionaries didn't invent this. They inherited it.

Look back at Jefferson's reading list. His favorite was *"the best elementary book of the principles of government, as founded in natural right, which has ever been published in any language."*

That was Algernon Sidney's *Discourses Concerning Government*.

Sidney knew liberty had one source, and it didn't come from a throne.

"The Liberties of Nations are from God and Nature, not from Kings."

As Montesquieu pointed out, even human laws written to protect rights are merely drawing on natural law.

"Antecedent to the above-mentioned laws are those of nature; so called because they derive their force entirely from our frame and existence."

Jean-Jacques Burlamaqui explained why it is called "natural," emphasizing that it is irrevocably grounded in our humanity.

"Natural law is that which so necessarily agrees with the nature and state of man, that without observing its maxims, the peace and happiness of society can never be preserved. As this law has an essential agreeableness with the constitution of human nature, the knowledge thereof may be attained merely by the light of reason; and hence it is called natural."

But even these enlightenment thinkers were building on the work of the ancients. Over 2000 years earlier, Aristotle established that it exists whether you agree with it, or not.

"That is natural which has the same validity everywhere, and does not depend on our accepting or rejecting it."

Cicero built on this foundation - true and natural law is an eternal, divine standard that applies to everyone, across all time.

"There is a true law, a right reason, conformable to nature, universal, unchangeable, eternal, whose commands urge us to duty, and whose prohibitions restrain us from evil.".

"It is not one thing at Rome and another at Athens; one thing to-day and another to-morrow; but in all times and nations this universal law must for ever reign, eternal and imperishable."

And true law, "conformable to nature," cannot be changed or legitimately ignored by any human government.

"This law cannot be contradicted by any other law, and is not liable either to derogation or abrogation."

"It is the sovereign master and emperor of all beings. God himself is its author, - its promulgator, - its enforcer."

PURSUIT

Samuel von Pufendorf laid out the progression - humanity starts in a state of nature, and the rules in that state are directly from their Creator. That is the foundation of liberty.

"Now those who live in the natural state have this particular right, that they are subject and responsible to none but God. From which standpoint that state is called natural liberty."

Burlamaqui defined exactly what that looks like. It's grounded entirely in property rights and self-ownership.

"Natural liberty is the right, which nature gives to all mankind, of disposing of their persons and property, after the manner they judge most convenient to their happiness."

He built this on a precursor to the modern-day non-aggression principle: exercise your rights however you see fit, so long as you don't violate the rights of others.

"On condition of their acting within the limits of the law of nature, and of their not abusing it to the prejudice of other men. To this right of liberty there is a reciprocal obligation corresponding, by which the law of nature binds all mankind to respect the liberty of other men, and not to disturb them in the use they make of it, so long as they do not abuse it."

Decades before Burlamaqui, John Locke had already tied natural liberty to the pursuit of happiness.

"As therefore the highest perfection of intellectual nature lies in a careful and constant pursuit of true and solid happiness, so the care of ourselves, that we mistake not imaginary for real happiness, is the necessary foundation of our liberty."

The whole point, he wrote, is to be free from outside influence and control.

"The stronger ties we have to an unalterable pursuit of happiness in general, which is our greatest good, and which, as such, our desires always follow, the more are we free from any necessary determination of our will to any particular action."

Building on this in the Colonies, Rev. John Wise emphasized that happiness is defined solely by the individual.

"Every Man has a Prerogative to Judge for himself, viz. What shall be most for his Behoof, Happiness and Well-being."

Put it all together, and you have the basis for what might be the most famous phrase in the Declaration of Independence.

"We hold these truths to be self-evident, that all men are created equal, that they are endowed by their Creator with certain unalienable Rights, that among these are Life, Liberty and the pursuit of Happiness."

CONSENT

Two years earlier, Jefferson captured the entire natural rights view in a single, uncompromising line.

"A free people [claim] their rights, as derived from the laws of nature, and not as the gift of their chief magistrate."

With natural law and natural liberty at the top of the food chain, and government at the bottom, Grotius delivered the logical result: The consent of the governed is what's required to make government laws legitimate.

"The Mother of Civil Law is that very Obligation which arises from Consent, which deriving its Force from the Law of Nature, Nature may be called as it were, the Great Grandmother of this Law also."

That principle of consent also found a prominent place in the Declaration of Independence.

"To secure these rights, Governments are instituted among Men, deriving their just powers from the consent of the governed."

Almost a decade earlier, John Dickinson tied consent and happiness together - through property rights.

"Let these truths be indelibly impressed on our minds----that we cannot be happy, without being free----that we cannot be free, without being secure in our property----that we cannot be secure in our property, if, without our consent, others may, as by right, take it away."

John Locke took that entire philosophical system and turned it into a mandate. Like Cicero before him, he held that no government has the legitimate authority to take away your natural rights.

"The obligations of the law of nature cease not in society, but only in many cases are drawn closer, and have by human laws known penalties annexed to them, to inforce their observation. Thus the law of nature stands as an eternal rule to all men, legislators as well as others."

Writing under the pseudonym Philalethes more than three decades before the Declaration, Elisha Williams clarified the ultimate purpose of that rule - government exists to protect life, liberty and property.

"The great end of civil government, is the preservation of their persons, their liberties and estates, or their property."

Governments, however, have a habit of ignoring rules that limit their power. But as James Otis, Jr. made clear, just because governments historically violate rights doesn't mean they acquire the **right** to do so. A precedent of abuse does not create legitimacy.

"But if every prince since Nimrod had been a tyrant, it would not prove a ***right*** *to tyrannize. There can be no prescription old enough to supersede the law of nature, and the grant of GOD almighty; who has given to all men a natural right to be* ***free****, and they have it ordinarily in their power to make themselves so, if they please."*

Otis set the stage for the core questions that naturally follow: who decides when this "eternal rule" is violated? And what needs to be done in response?

Chapter 3

SOVEREIGNTY

"*The fundamental principle of the revolution.*"

That's how James Madison described the monumental shift in how the people viewed sovereignty. Sir Francis Bernard defined it as final power and authority, *"not subordinate to or dependent upon any earthly power."*

All through history, most people lived under a system where government held this power. But as Madison pointed out, the American Revolution changed that.

Completely.

THE BRITISH VIEW

In 1764, Bernard, the royal governor of Massachusetts, laid out the British position on sovereignty - starting with a definition.

"In all imperial states there resides somewhere or other an absolute power, which we will call the sovereignty."

With the definition set, Bernard explained exactly where that power lived: in the government itself.

"The Sovereignty of Great Britain is in the King in Parliament; that is, in the King, acting with the advice and consent of the Lords and Commons (by their Representatives), assembled in the Parliament of Great Britain."

The practical conclusion? Government determined the extent of its own power. That meant its power was unlimited, just as Bernard described.

"The King in Parliament has the sole right of legislation, and the supreme superintendency of the government; and, in this plentitude of power, is absolute, uncontrollable, and accountable to none; and therefore in a political sense, can do no wrong."

The British had a constitutional system, but not the kind Americans understand today. The constitution was unwritten, and no significant distinction existed between "the constitution or frame of government" and "the system of laws" enacted by the government.

In short, every act of Parliament became part of the structure, the unwritten British constitution. Because Parliament was sovereign, anything it did was, by definition, constitutional.

In the British view, it was an absurdity to argue an act of Parliament was "unconstitutional."

And as Bernard explained, the British applied this exact standard to the colonies - despite the fact that the colonists had no representation in Parliament.

"The Parliament of Great Britain, as well from its rights of Sovereignty as from occasional exigencies, has a right to make laws for, and impose taxes upon, its subjects in its external dominations, although they are not represented in such Parliament."

Colonists argued they had traditionally exercised legislative power over their own internal and local affairs. Bernard dismissed this entirely. Local control wasn't a right, it was a British gift. And it could be revoked at will.

"A separate Legislation is not an absolute right of British subjects residing out of the seat of Empire; it may or may not be allowed, and has or has not been granted, according to the circumstances of the community."

In practice, the British system operated like what we'd today call a "living, breathing" constitution - where the government defined its own limits and had the power to change those limits as it decided.

THE AMERICAN EVOLUTION

The American Revolution was built on the opposite view, but it was an understanding that evolved and expanded over time.

In *The Rights of the British Colonies Asserted and Proved*, James Otis Jr. acknowledged, as Bernard did, that sovereignty must lie somewhere.

"An original supreme sovereign, absolute, and uncontrollable earthly power must exist in and preside over every society; from whose final decisions there can be no appeal but directly to Heaven."

Unlike the British view, he held that sovereignty belonged to the people, not the government.

"It is therefore originally and ultimately in the people."

But even here, Otis was hedging. His view represented an early shift in understanding, not a complete one. Despite confirming that sovereignty resides in the people, he still accepted parliamentary **supremacy** in practice.

"Therefore let the parliament lay what burthens they please on us, we must, it is our duty to submit and patiently bear them, till they will be pleased to relieve us."

Even with this contradiction, Otis set the foundation - and it didn't take long for others to build on it. The following year, delegates from nine colonies gathered at the Stamp Act Congress of 1765. Like Otis, they affirmed *"all due subordination"* to Parliament. But unlike Otis, they drew a very specific line - rejecting Parliamentary power to lay internal taxes at all. The historical precedent wasn't a British gift that could be revoked. It was a constitutional line that could not be crossed.

"No taxes ever have been or can be constitutionally imposed on them but by their respective legislatures."

The colonies had moved past the contradiction. But they still didn't fully explain why the line existed where it did.

Dickinson's Division

It was John Dickinson - the primary author of the Resolutions of the Stamp Act Congress - who took the torch and advanced the argument further.

Written in late 1767 and published as a series into early 1768, his *Letters from a Farmer in Pennsylvania* struck directly at the British view that sovereignty must be singular and indivisible within the central government itself. Dickinson insisted it could be divided, and the line was external versus internal.

First, he argued that Parliament held final authority over external trade and regulations.

"The parliament unquestionably possesses a legal authority to regulate the trade of Great Britain, and all her colonies. Such an authority is essential to the relation between a mother country and her colonies; and necessary for the common good of all."

Then he flat out rejected the opposing view - that Parliament had no authority at all.

"He who considers these provinces as states distinct from the British Empire, has very slender notions of justice, or of their interests. We are but parts of a whole; and therefore there must exist a power somewhere, to preside, and preserve the connection in due order. This power is lodged in the parliament; and we are as much dependent on Great Britain, as a perfectly free people can be on another."

That was the limit. The people were sovereign over their own internal matters, whether through their own elected assemblies or otherwise - including taxation. And that meant all taxation - even external duties dressed up as trade regulations. When Parliament tried to cross that line, he said it acted outside its authority entirely.

"To this I answer, with a total denial of the power of parliament to lay upon these colonies any "tax" whatever."

Dickinson continued, again rejecting the notion that local legislation was a British gift that could be revoked.

He argued that Parliament had never taxed the colonies for revenue, never passed a law to do so, and never suggested it would or could. This meant they never intended to have the power, regardless of what anyone in Britain claimed to the contrary.

"I have looked over every statute relating to these colonies, from their first settlement to this time; and I find every one of them founded on this principle, till the Stamp Act administration. All before, are calculated to regulate trade, and preserve or promote a mutually beneficial intercourse between the several constituent parts of the empire; and though many of them imposed duties on trade, yet those duties were always imposed with design to restrain the commerce of one part, that was injurious to another, and thus to promote the general welfare. The raising of a revenue thereby was never intended."

Although Dickinson accepted Parliament's authority over external trade regulation as legitimate, the principle was set: sovereignty could be divided, and Parliament's reach had limits.

When it went beyond them - like internal taxation - it was as a usurpation of power, and a violation of the unwritten British constitution.

Samuel Adams and James Otis explained the hierarchy in the *Massachusetts Circular Letter*. The Constitution was supreme over acts of government, not the other way around.

"In all free states the constitution is fixed, and as the supreme legislative derives its power and authority from the constitution, it cannot overleap the bounds of it without destroying its own foundation; that the constitution ascertains and limits both sovereignty and allegiance."

Franklin's Question

But this divided sovereignty approach was still not the complete view of the American Revolution.

Benjamin Franklin held a similar view to Dickinson, at least at first.

In 1766, testifying before the House of Commons, he accepted Parliament's unlimited power to regulate external trade.

"The authority of parliament was allowed to be valid in all laws, except such as should lay internal taxes. It was never disputed in laying duties to regulate commerce."

The British questioning him understood that this divided sovereignty position was just a step away from no sovereignty for Parliament at all. So when asked whether the colonists might eventually reject Parliament's external authority as well, his answer was a prophetic warning.

"At present they do not reason so, but in time they may possibly be convinced by these arguments."

Two years later, Franklin was in the process of being convinced himself. Writing a month after the *Circular Letter*, he rejected Dickinson's divided sovereignty as unworkable.

"The more I have thought and read on the subject the more I find myself confirmed in opinion, that no middle doctrine can be well maintained, I mean not clearly with intelligible arguments. Something might be made of either of the extremes; that Parliament has a power to make all laws for us, or that it has a power to make no laws for us."

No middle ground. Parliament either had absolute power over the colonies, or none at all. And Franklin was already leaning toward none.

"And I think the arguments for the latter more numerous and weighty than those for the former."

Jefferson's Complete View

Thomas Jefferson considered Dickinson's view - where *"England had a right to regulate our commerce, and to lay duties on it for the purposes of regulation, but not of raising revenue"* - to be an unacceptable *"half-way house."*

He was ready to completely renounce that, even though most of Virginia's political elite still accepted it in 1774. This included, as he recalled in his autobiography, *"Randolph, the Lees, Nicholas, Pendleton."*

He later described his opposition to the divided sovereignty view, *"but for this ground there was no foundation in compact, in any acknoleged principles of colonisation, nor in reason."*

In his draft instructions for the Virginia delegates to the First Continental Congress in 1774, later reprinted as *A Summary*

View of the Rights of British America, he referred to Colonial legislatures as *"free and independent."*

After reciting a long list of *"arbitrary measures,"* he continued, writing that he didn't consider them nullities because they were just bad policy.

"We do not point out to his majesty the injustice of these acts, with intent to rest on that principle the cause of their nullity."

You can't call something a nullity - a theft of power - if the government holds sovereignty. And that's where the rubber met the road with the American view of sovereignty. Thomas Jefferson made that case next.

"The true ground on which we declare these acts void is, that the British parliament has no right to exercise authority over us."

At the time, Jefferson found few allies for this position. As he later recalled, of the old guard, only his mentor and law teacher George Wythe was on board.

"I had never been able to get any one to agree with me but mr Wythe. he concurred in it from the first dawn of the question."

But despite the unwillingness of the First Virginia Convention to take Jefferson's view as their official position, Edmund Randolph recalled there was still plenty of admiration to go around.

"I distinctly recollect the applause bestowed on the most of them, when they were read to a large company at the house of Peyton Randolph, to whom they were addressed."

But the applause wasn't universal, because Dickinson's position was still held up as the gold standard.

"Of all the approbation was not equal. From the celebrated letters of the Pennsylvanian Farmer (John Dickinson) we had been instructed to bow to the external taxation of parliament."

Still, even a rejected argument can crack a foundation. When they questioned Franklin in 1766, the British feared this exact shift. Randolph noted that this was exactly what was happening.

"But this composition of Mr. Jefferson, shook this conceeded principle."

The question at the time wasn't whether Jefferson was right or wrong. It was whether everyone was ready to acknowledge it. And the answer was mostly along generational lines.

"The young ascended with Mr. Jefferson to the source of those rights, the old required time for consideration before they could tread this lofty ground, which, if it had not been abandoned, at least had not been fully occupied throughout America."

Jefferson himself recalled that the principle was ahead of its time.

"It was read generally by the members, approved by many, but thought too bold for the present state of things"

But "too bold" didn't mean ignored. Even without official backing from the Convention, Jefferson's argument found powerful allies willing to spread it.

George Washington pledged three shillings and nine pence for the publication of what he called *"Mr Jefferson's Bill of Rights,"* and after others pitched in as well, that began the widespread distribution of his "Summary View."

It was first published in Williamsburg as a pamphlet, but soon after, presses in Philadelphia, London, and beyond followed suit. By the summer of 1775, Jefferson's reputation arrived at the Second Continental Congress before he did.

Delegate Samuel Ward, for example, wrote to his brother Henry, Secretary of Rhode Island, with his first impression of *"the famous Mr. Jefferson,"* whom he described as *"a very sensible, spirited, fine fellow - and by the pamphlet he wrote last summer, he certainly is one."*

THE RESULT

But while pamphleteers and delegates debated the limits and location of sovereignty, John Adams later argued the question had already been answered - in practice - nearly a decade before Jefferson ever put ink to paper.

The colonists' refusal to comply with the Stamp Act in 1765 wasn't just resistance. It was the Jeffersonian view, fully operational, before anyone had articulated it.

"Here were already two Nations directly and explicitly at issue concerning their fundamental Laws. For if the Sovereignty of the Empire was vested in Parliament, a Denial of its Right to tax the Colonies was a Declaration of total Independence on Parliament."

In short, the British view held that all power was originally lodged in government. And that same government would determine its own limits. While some had challenged that view over more than a century, it persisted. Even Burlamaqui, writing in 1748, went too far for the British - he held that sovereignty in government was not permanent.

"If the sovereign, utterly forgetful of the end for which he was entrusted with the sovereignty, applied it to a quite contrary purpose, and thus became an enemy to the state; the sovereignty returns (ipso facto) to the nation, who, in that case, can act towards the person, who was their sovereign, in the manner they think most agreeable to their security and interests."

That's what made the American view so radical. As George Mason put it, government never held that original power in the first place.

"In all our associations; in all our agreements let us never lose sight of this fundamental maxim—that all power was originally lodged in, and consequently is derived from, the people. We should wear it as a breastplate, and buckle it on as our armour."

If all power starts with the people, then any system built on governmental sovereignty has a name. Thomas Paine gave it one - despotism.

"In despotic monarchies (such as the British government) power is lodged in a single person, or sovereign. His will is law; which he declares, alters or revokes as he pleases, without being accountable to any power for so doing."

The American system, he wrote, was built on the opposite foundation.

"In republics, such as those established in America, the sovereign power, or the power over which there is no control, and which controls all others, remains where nature placed it-in the people; for the people in America are the fountain of power."

This radical change in how the people understood sovereignty found its ultimate expression in the Declaration of Independence, affirming that government power is derived from the consent of the people.

"That to secure these rights, Governments are instituted among Men, deriving their just powers from the consent of the governed, – That whenever any Form of Government becomes destructive of these ends, it is the Right of the People to alter or to abolish it, and to institute new Government, laying its foundation on such principles and organizing its powers in such form, as to them shall seem most likely to effect their Safety and Happiness."

This ultimate act of sovereignty - that the people can alter or even abolish government at will - shattered the British conception of sovereignty.

James Madison recognized this American view of sovereignty as the foundation of their independence.

"The fundamental principle on which our independence itself was declared."

Once the people understand that they hold final authority, every act of government faces a question. Was that power given - or was it taken?

Chapter 4

ARBITRARY POWER

"The curse and scandal of human nature."

That's how James Otis, Jr. described arbitrary power. It wasn't just a sign of tyranny, or a step toward it. It was the very definition of it.

That was the danger John Adams later described - the threat that opened their eyes and changed their minds.

And that understanding pervades the Declaration of Independence.

DEFINED

James Otis Jr. defined it this way in 1762:

"arbitrary; which in plain English means no more than to do as one pleases."

Whenever a government acts beyond the limits of its constitution, it is arbitrary. It is lawless.

It doesn't matter who wields that power, whether a king in France or Great Britain, or anyone on Earth. The power itself is the great threat.

"That arbitrary government implies the worst of temporal evils, or at least the continual danger of them is certain. That a man would be pretty equally subjected to these under every arbitrary government, is clear."

For Otis, arbitrary power wasn't just dangerous. As the British showed by violating their own unwritten constitution, it was vile and corrupt.

"A greater difference on this side the Grave cannot be found, than that which subsists between British subjects, and the slaves of tyranny."

SPREADING THE PRINCIPLE

This rejection of arbitrary power didn't begin or end with James Otis Jr. It echoed across the continent in speeches, resolutions, and revolutionary writings.

It also rang from the pulpit. Take Stephen Johnson's warning from Connecticut.

"When leaders of administration openly adopt arbitrary and oppressive measures in a free state, government is corrupt as in its fountain, and the foundations of it are shaken."

Mercy Otis Warren went so far as to call arbitrary power *"disgusting to every man of virtue."*

After passage of the Coercive Acts and the subsequent blockade of the Boston harbor in 1774, delegates from twelve colonies met in Philadelphia to plan their response. The First Continental Congress named arbitrary power as the very reason they convened.

"The good people of the several colonies... justly alarmed at these arbitrary proceedings of parliament and administration, have severally elected, constituted, and appointed deputies to meet... in order to obtain such establishment, as that their religion, laws, and liberties, may not be subverted."

The following week, they made it even more explicit – unanimously passing John Jay's *Address to the People of Great Britain*, which expressly named arbitrary power as unconstitutional.

"That we think the Legislature of Great Britain is not authorized by the Constitution to establish a Religion fraught with sanguinary and impious tenets, or to erect an arbitrary form of Government in any quarter of the globe. These rights we, as well as you, deem sacred; and yet, sacred as they are, they have, with many others, been repeatedly and flagrantly violated."

Just weeks before the first shots at Lexington and Concord, Joseph Warren delivered one of the strongest public condemnations of arbitrary power.

"Savages, and death with torture were far less terrible than slavery: nothing was so much the object of their abhorrence as a tyrant's power: they knew that it was more safe to dwell with man in his most unpolished state, - than in a country where arbitrary power prevails."

This wasn't just passionate rhetoric. It was principle, a line in the sand. And no one stated that principle more clearly than Samuel Adams and James Otis, Jr.

"The legislative has no right to absolute arbitrary power over the lives and fortunes of the people."

FOUNDATION

These views long predated the Revolution. From the lessons of ancient history in Athens, Rome and beyond, to the thinkers of the Enlightenment, the warnings came through loud and clear.

In *The Oceana*, James Harrington referred to government based on arbitrary power as one *"without any bounds,"* and therefore, any such system *"fully amounts to tyranny."*

John Locke drew a similar line between lawful rule and power without limits.

"Absolute arbitrary power, or governing without settled standing laws, can neither of them consist with the ends of society and government."

Writing as the *Whig Examiner* in the early 18th century, Joseph Addison, who later became famous in the colonies for his play, *Cato, a Tragedy,* framed the essential question of his day: limited government, or tyranny?

"Whether our Prince be obliged by our constitution to act according to law, or whether he be arbitrary and despotical."

Thomas Gordon took things further and mocked the very idea of "law" under arbitrary power. The result isn't just bad laws, it's a race to the bottom. Each arbitrary decree is more oppressive, more abusive, more destructive than the last.

"Thus in arbitrary countries, a law aged two days is an old law; and no law is suffered to be a standing law, but such as are found by long experience to be so very bad, and so thoroughly destructive, that human malice, and all the arts of a tyrant's court, cannot make them worse."

It should be no surprise that Montesquieu saw a love of arbitrary power in every tyrant throughout history.

"Has it ever been heard that kings were not fond of monarchy, or that despotic princes hated arbitrary power?"

THE DECLARATION

There was also another name for it. Every arbitrary act was an act of usurpation, as John Locke defined it - stolen power.

"Usurpation is the exercise of power, which another hath a right to."

Pick up a dictionary in 1773, like Samuel Johnson's widely-read *Dictionary of the English Language*, and the definition for usurpation hits even harder.

"Forcible, unjust, illegal seizure or possession."

That is precisely the term they used when they made their case to the world in the Declaration of Independence.

Most people call the list of charges against the king "grievances," but that word isn't even in the document.

Not once.

What is?

"A long train of abuses and ***usurpations****."*

And:

"A history of repeated injuries and ***usurpations****."*

The Declaration wasn't a mere protest against bad leadership or temporary policy disputes. In his rough draft, Jefferson didn't leave anything open to interpretation. It was an indictment of a deliberate, calculated train of stolen power, destroying the constitution and rendering the entire system arbitrary.

"But when a long train of abuses & usurpations, begun at a distinguished period, & pursuing invariably the same object, evinces

a design to subject them to arbitrary power, it is their right, it is their duty, to throw off such government."

Benjamin Franklin suggested a change – from "arbitrary power" to "absolute Despotism." But the underlying principle didn't change at all.

Jefferson made the standard clear: not every usurpation, and not every exercise of arbitrary power, is enough to justify throwing off a government.

"Prudence, indeed, will dictate that Governments long established should not be changed for light and transient causes."

That bears repeating. They weren't calling for separation over every act of usurpation. They were warning what to do when usurpation becomes the design, when the system itself becomes arbitrary.

A surefire sign that the system is arbitrary is the presence of the *"scourge of the innocent,"* a standing army.

Chapter 5

STANDING ARMIES

March 5, 1770. The Boston Massacre. British regulars fired on a crowd. Five people died.

Tragic, yes. Predictable, absolutely.

On the fourth anniversary of the massacre, John Hancock explained that the deadly outcome was inevitable.

"It was easy to foresee the consequences which so naturally followed upon sending troops into America to enforce obedience to acts of the British Parliament, which neither God nor man ever empowered them to make."

Opposition to standing armies was almost universal. It's hard to overstate how reviled they were.

Joseph Warren held they *"always endanger the liberty"* of the people.

Not sometimes. Not even most of the time.

Always.

Jonathan Mason called them the *"scourge of the innocent."*

And the Declaration of Independence famously decried the King for one of his greatest abuses, *"He has kept among us, in times of peace, Standing Armies without the Consent of our legislatures."*

TOOL OF TYRANNY

Arbitrary power doesn't enforce itself. It needs muscle, and as John Dickinson made clear, the preferred tool of tyrants throughout history had always been a standing army: *"that single engine of arbitrary power."*

Despite the claims of those in power, Simeon Howard knew that framing standing armies solely as a matter of "safety" was always a ruse.

"Rulers of an arbitrary disposition, have ever endeavored to have a standing army at their command, under a pretence indeed, of being for the safety of the state, though really with a view of giving efficacy to their orders."

In his sermon celebrating the repeal of the Stamp Act, Jonathan Mayhew made the case that much of the opposition to the hated tax stemmed from the fear that the funds would be used to pay for a standing army.

"Others were anxious, because they imagined, with how much, or how little reason you will best judge, that the money was to be chiefly applied towards maintaining a standing army in America."

John Dickinson was clear: this concern about taxes being used to fund a standing army wasn't paranoia. It was pattern recognition.

"These facts are sufficient to support what I have said. It is true, that all the mischiefs apprehended by our ancestors from a standing army and excise, have not yet happened: But it does not follow from this, that they will not happen. The inside of a house may catch fire, and the most valuable apartments be ruined, before the flames burst out. The question in these cases is not, what evil has actually

attended particular measures - but, what evil, in the nature of things, is likely to attend them."

Like Howard after him, Mayhew explained that the people didn't fall for the "it's for your safety" trick. They knew it was just a tool to enforce compliance with arbitrary power.

"...not so much to defend and secure the colonies from enemies, of whom they had none, except the aforesaid fowlers, as to awe the colonies themselves into an implicit obedience to ministerial measures, however unjust or execrable in their nature."

As Benjamin Hichborn forcefully argued, the very existence of a standing army means someone is enforcing arbitrary power.

"Every military force must necessarily imply a right of exercising an arbitrary power, so far as respects the objects against which it is to be directed; and what will be the objects against which it will be in constant exercise in proportion to its extent, we may collect from the experience of ages, and the well-known source of human actions."

Jonathan Williams Austin may have summed up their view best: Standing armies don't uphold the law, they destroy it.

"We shall ever find it an unalterable maxim of princes, who in time of peace keep up a standing force, however they may call them the protectors of law, the end is to subvert those laws and render the constitution useless."

GUARANTEED

This wasn't just theory. The American Revolutionaries watched it play out firsthand. For them, the greatest act of arbitrary power was the Declaratory Act of 1766, which claimed unlimited power over the Colonies *"in all cases whatsoever."*

John Hancock recognized this as the foundation for all the other individual acts of arbitrary power that followed.

"They have declared that they have, ever had, and of right ought ever to have, full power to make laws of sufficient validity to bind the colonies in all cases whatever: They have exercised this pretended right by imposing a tax upon us without our consent;"

But that tax wasn't going to enforce itself. And that's where the standing army came in.

"And lest we should shew some reluctance at parting with our property, her fleets and armies are sent to inforce their mad pretensions."

Hancock was far from alone in this understanding. Warren traced it right back to the root cause of the Massacre. The British knew they couldn't convince the people to submit, so they did what all empires do - more arbitrary power.

"As it was soon found that this taxation could not be supported by reason and argument, it seemed necessary that one act of oppression should be enforced by another."

And that next act of oppression was, of course, sending in the troops.

"A standing army was established among us in a time of peace."

He knew they weren't there for window dressing, either.

"Namely for the enforcement of obedience to acts which, upon fair examination, appeared to be unjust and unconstitutional."

And once the occupying army arrived? Warren understood exactly what Hancock did: The terrible result was guaranteed - because it was part of a well-known formula.

"When the people on the one part, considered the army as sent to enslave them, and the army on the other, were taught to look on the people as in a state of rebellion, it was but just to fear the most disagreeable consequences. Our fears, we have seen, were but too well grounded."

GRAVEYARD OF REPUBLICS

The reason this was so widely expected, as Austin explained, was that history had already provided the proof.

"Philosophers and statesmen have shewn how dangerous standing armies must be in a free state, and every page in the volume of mankind confirms the melancholy account."

Warren pointed to the graveyard of republics to show that this was a lesson written in the ruins of history.

"The ruinous consequences of standing armies to free communities, may be seen in the histories of SYRACUSE, ROME, and many other once flourishing states; some of which have now scarce a name!"

Take ancient Syracuse, for example. Thomas Gordon explained the descent, which started with a supposed hero: Agathocles.

"Agathocles fought successfully for the city of Syracuse, and as successfully against it; and having defended the citizens against their enemies, he afterwards shewed himself their greatest, by killing in one great massacre all the chief and best of them, and by crowning himself tyrant over all the rest."

And then there's Rome, the most famous example of all. James Lovell invoked the classic story: a popular general, a loyal army, and a republic brought to its knees.

"Caesar by the length of his command in Gaul got the affections of his army, marched to Rome, overthrew the state, and made himself perpetual dictator."

But, as Peter Thacher warned, you don't have to start with legions to destroy a republic.

"From small beginnings, and under spacious pretences, they will use

a standing military force, the most successfull engine ever yet weilded by the hand of lawless domination."

Lovell issued a timeless reminder: the original blueprint started with a single, small step - a personal guard of just fifty men.

"Athens once was free; a citizen, a favorite of the people, by an artful story gained a trifling guard of fifty men; ambition taught him ways to enlarge that number; he destroyed the commonwealth and made himself the tyrant of the Athenians."

That "artful story" had a name: Pisistratus. As David Hume documented, he staged a false flag, an attack on himself, to build a guard that became a standing army.

"Pisistratus, the Athenian, who cut and wounded his own body; and making the people believe, that his enemies had committed the violence, obtained a guard for his person."

Gordon wrote that this started extremely small - with a seemingly pathetic force, just fifty men, armed only with wooden clubs. But that was all that was needed to get the ball rolling towards total tyranny.

"Pisistratus, having procured from the city of Athens fifty fellows armed only with cudgels, for the security of his person from false and lying dangers, improved them into an army, and by it enslaved that free state."

BRITISH HISTORY

This wasn't just ancient history. Thacher pointed to a core part of their own history, their own heritage.

"There is no need of recurring to the ancient histories of Greece and Rome, for instances of these truths. The British nation, once famous for its attachment to freedom, and enthusiastically jealous of its

rights, is now become a great tame beast, which fetches and carries for any minister who pleases to employ it."

Josiah Quincy traced English opposition to standing armies all the way back to the reign of Richard II at the end of the 14th century.

"After the Romans quitted the island of Britain, the first appearance of a standing army was under Richard the second. The suppression of his enemies in Ireland calling him out of England, his subjects, seized the opportunity and dethroned him."

Despite that victory against such a small start, John Dickinson urged the people to oppose even *"slight beginnings"* - with the reign of Henry VII being a powerful example why. Starting with just fifty men, it's almost as if Henry saw Pisistratus as a model to copy - rather than a warning.

"Henry the seventh was the first monarch of that kingdom, who established a standing body of armed men. This was a band of 50 archers, called yeomen of the guard: And this institution, notwithstanding the smallness of the number, was, to prevent discontent, 'disguised under the pretence of majesty and grandeur.'"

That, of course, was just the start. The force grew in the years that followed, serving as an ominous warning for what Dickinson was writing about in 1767.

"In 1684, the standing forces were so much augmented, that Rapin says - 'The King, in order to make his people fully sensible of their new slavery, affected to muster his troops, which amounted to 4000 well armed and disciplined men.' I think our army, at this time, consists of more than seventy regiments."

Quincy emphasized the history everyone already knew. That tiny force of fifty, which grew to four thousand over the years, gave the Crown the power to imprison subjects without trial, and even kill them, effectively ending the protection of common law. It was rule by the sword instead of the law. Violence and bloodshed in place of justice.

Thomas Gordon documented what was likely the most famous British example, wrapped in the rhetoric of freedom.

"Oliver Cromwell headed an Army which pretended to fight for Liberty, and by that Army became a bloody Tyrant; as I once saw a Hawk very generously rescue a Turtle Dove from the Persecution of two Crows, and then eat him up himself."

Cromwell wasn't the exception. For Gordon, he was part of a universal rule.

"Tis certain, that all Parts of Europe which are enslaved, have been enslaved by Armies, and 'tis absolutely impossible, that any Nation which keeps them amongst themselves, can long preserve their Liberties; nor can any Nation perfectly lose their Liberties, who are without such Guests."

But the most dangerous "guests" - Quincy warned - weren't always outsiders.

"An invasion and conquest by mere strangers and foreigners are neither so formidable or disgraceful as the establishment of a standing army under colour description of the municipal law of the land. Thus Roman armies were more terrible to the Roman colonies, than an 'enemy's army.'"

SUBVERTING THE MILITIA

If all that wasn't enough, standing armies also have another "feature" that made them the ultimate threat to a free state.

Lovell warned that they compete with citizen militias, driving them into decay.

"I must not omit to mention one more bad tendency: 'tis this, - a

standing force leads to a total neglect of militias, or tends greatly to discourage them."

That's because, as Dr. Thomas Welsh explained, when standing armies are established, people tend to succumb to complacency - deferring their own defense to a professional class.

"When communities have so far mistaken their interest, as to commit the defence of every thing valuable in life to a standing army; the love of ease will scarcely permit them to reassume the unpleasing task of defending themselves."

Lovell noted this is dangerous precisely because the **true** defense of any society is the militia.

"The true strength and safety of every commonwealth or limited monarchy, is the bravery of its freeholders, its militia. By brave militias they rise to grandeur, and they come to ruin by a mercenary army. This is founded on historical facts; and the same causes will, in similar circumstances, forever produce the same effects."

Welsh explained why: The militia - the people themselves - they have a strong incentive to defend their own country and their own liberty against all enemies, foreign and domestic.

"A militia is the most natural defence of a free state, from invasion and tyranny: they who compose the militia, are the proprietors of the soil; and who are so likely to defend it, as they who have received it from their ancestors - acquired it by their labor - or obtained it by their valour?"

John Hancock reinforced this point. A militia isn't fighting for a paycheck - they're free people defending everything they love.

"They fight for their houses, their lands, for their wives, their children, for all who claim the tenderest names, and are held dearest in their hearts, they fight pro aris & focis, for their liberty, and for themselves, and for their God."

Flip it around, and Simeon Howard explained why a professional standing army has a natural tendency to dominate rather than protect.

"When there is any difference between rulers and subjects, they will generally be on the side of the former, and ready to assist them in oppressing and enslaving the latter. For though they are really servants of the people, and paid by them; yet this is not commonly done in their name; but in the name of the supreme magistrate."

Chain of command, he noted, tends to override a duty to serve the people themselves - a dangerous tool in the hands of a person willing to overstep the Constitution.

"The KING'S BREAD, and the KING'S SERVICE, are familiar expressions among soldiers, and tend to make them consider him as their only master, and prefer his personal interest to that of the people. So that an army may be the means, in the hands of a wicked and oppressive sovereign, of overturning the constitution of a country, and establishing the most intolerable despotism."

THE BILL COMES DUE

With these lessons from centuries of history, Americans watched with alarm as 1763 brought a familiar danger to their own shores. At the end of the French and Indian War, the British decided to station ten thousand troops for "protection," serving an added bonus for the Empire: a jobs program to keep many troops from being out of work.

A standing army isn't cheap. So the British decided the colonies would pay for it. That unleashed a wave of taxes: the Sugar Act, the Stamp Act, the Townshend Acts, and more.

John Adams saw the dangerous cycle: first the army, then the taxes, all based on unconstitutional power.

"We have the mortification to observe one Act of Parliament after another passed for the express purpose of raising a revenue from us; to see our money continually collecting from us without our consent, by an authority in the constitution of which we have no share, and over which we have no kind of influence or controul."

Adams pushed the indictment further: their money was not only being stolen, but actively used to pay for the tools of their own oppression.

"To see the little circulating cash that remained among us for the support of our trade, from time to time transmitted to a distant country, never to return, or what in our estimation is worse, if possible, appropriated to the maintenance of swarms of Officers and Pensioners in idleness and luxury, whose example has a tendency to corrupt our morals, and whose arbitrary dispositions will trample on our rights."

This creates a cycle rooted in war that James Madison later decried as the "most to be dreaded" enemy of liberty.

"War is the parent of armies; from these proceed debts and taxes; and armies, and debts, and taxes are the known instruments for bringing the many under the domination of the few."

This cycle was likely already obvious to John Dickinson when he issued this reminder in 1774: Even the greatest empires have destroyed themselves through a standing army.

*"**Great-Britain** ought not to forget, that **Rome** was ruined by keeping standing armies in her provinces."*

This history was no secret. When Benjamin Franklin repeated this near the end of the War for Independence, he added a timeless warning: Despite knowing this truth, the hubris of those in power guarantees they'll eventually meet the same fate.

"Empires, by Pride & Folly & Extravagance, ruin themselves like Individuals."

Understanding all this, it should be no surprise to learn that the Founders and Old Revolutionaries, as expressed here by Thomas Dawes, viewed a standing army and a free society as totally incompatible - like oil and water.

"Hence it is that in free states as such there is no such thing as a perpetual standing army."

But preventing it from becoming established as the **system** - or in the words of the Declaration of Independence - part of a *"design to reduce them under absolute Despotism"* - means recognizing each and every step towards it, no matter how small.

That includes a seemingly innocuous guard of just a few dozen men, or even a small act of arbitrary power that will require enforcement by violence in the future.

Chapter 6

PRECEDENT

"The people of the U. S. owe their Independence & their liberty, to the wisdom of descrying in the minute tax of 3 pence on tea, the magnitude of the evil comprized in the precedent."

Precedent.

Going all the way back to ancient Greece, they knew the score: once government usurps power, no matter how "minute" it might be, it keeps growing and it never gives it back.

As James Madison explained so clearly, the people understood this lesson burned in the pages of history.

Recognizing the danger in even a single step is the only way to be free.

PATH TO TYRANNY

"One of the vilest systems that can be set up."

That's how Thomas Paine described government by precedent:

when government uses power not because it's authorized, but because someone else got away with it first.

No constitution. No limits. Just repetition and raw power.

One act becomes two. Two becomes twenty. In no time, power is no longer delegated – it's simply arbitrary and assumed.

James Otis, Jr. explained that this is the usual process. Rather than a single event, the path to tyranny is a long, slow descent.

"A free government never degenerated into tyranny all at once, it is the work of years."

John Adams described this expansion of power as relentless and ever-growing, like a deadly disease.

"The nature of the encroachment upon the American constitution is such, as to grow every day more and more encroaching. Like a cancer, it eats faster and faster every hour."

THE TRAP

The Roman historian Tacitus captured the danger in one powerful line from a speech by the Emperor Claudius. What is done today will be used as the basis for more in the future.

"What we are this day justifying by precedents, will be itself a precedent."

While the empire saw this as a positive - a tool to build and expand their power - John Dickinson and the American revolutionaries recognized it as the ultimate trap.

"Indeed we ought firmly to believe, what is an undoubted truth, confirmed by the unhappy experience of many states heretofore free, that unless the most watchful attention be exerted, a new servitude may be slipped upon us, under the sanction of usual and respectable terms."

First, he exposed how power-hungry politicians rarely declare themselves dictators. Instead, they cloak their schemes to look legitimate.

"All artful rulers, who strive to extend their power beyond its just limits, endeavor to give to their attempts as much semblance of legality as possible."

Then, he showed how precedent builds on precedent.

"Those who succeed them may venture to go a little further; for each new encroachment will be strengthened by a former."

And finally, he brought it full circle – directly citing Tacitus.

"'That which is now supported by examples, growing old, will become an example itself,' and thus support fresh usurpations."

Dickinson knew that when the people tolerate just one abuse of power, they have already lost. Government will always come for more, and the people will be more likely to allow it.

"When an act injurious to freedom has been once done, and the people bear it, the repetition of it is most likely to meet with submission."

Human nature and simple psychology explain why this works repeatedly throughout history. The people rationalize and accept more of the same.

"For as the mischief of the one was found to be tolerable, they will hope that of the second will prove so too; and they will not regard the infamy of the last, because they are stained with that of the first."

EMERGENCY POWER

Dickinson also knew the most dangerous word in politics: "emergency."

To prove his point, he reached back to Spain's transformation into a tyranny – all triggered by a single precedent.

"Spain was once free. Their cortes resembled our parliaments. No money could be raised on the subject, without their consent."

Picture that: a functioning representative government where the people controlled the purse strings. Then came the trap.

"One of their Kings having received a grant from them, to maintain a war against the Moors, desired, that if the sum which they had given, should not be sufficient, he might be allowed, ***for that emergency only****, to raise more money without assembling the Cortes."* [emphasis added]

Notice those words: "for that emergency only." Sounds familiar, doesn't it?

Dickinson described how some saw through this scheme.

"The request was violently opposed by the best and wisest men in the assembly."

But wisdom doesn't always win.

"It was, however, complied with by the votes of a majority; and this single concession was a PRECEDENT for other concessions of the like kind."

The result was catastrophic.

"Until at last the crown obtained a general power of raising money, in cases of necessity. From that period the Cortes ceased to be useful – the people ceased to be free."

From one emergency exception to permanent power. From free people to subjects.

All through a single precedent.

Samuel Adams identified the same pattern in France. The "fatal moment" came in 1439.

"France afterwards fell into the same snare."

King Charles VII asked the legislature, the Estates General, for emergency power to unilaterally fund a standing army for war against the British. They granted it, believing it was temporary. But as Thomas Gordon documented, once government could define *"great necessity,"* every subsequent problem became one.

"I have read somewhere, of the States of a country, who having wildly granted to their prince a power of raising money by his own authority, in cases of great necessity; every case, ever afterwards, was a case of great necessity; and his necessities multiplied so fast, that the whole wealth of the country was swallowed up to supply them."

Samuel Adams tracked how quickly things progressed across generations. Charles VII started with modest sums. His son Louis XI tripled the revenue. Their successors kept expanding the tax burden until they had confiscated everything.

"Charles the seventh, who began them, never rais'd annually more than one hundred and eighty thousand Pounds. His Son Lewis the eleventh almost trebled the Revenue; and since then, all that the Kingdom and People had, even to their Skins, has hardly been thought sufficient for their Kings."

These aren't random tragedies separated by centuries. They're the same story repeating. Because, as Dickinson explained, power operates on one iron principle. What it takes, it never gives back.

"Power is of a tenacious nature: What it seizes it will retain."

GOOD BEGINNINGS

Even those who recognize the dangers of this precedent trap often suspend their principles when the cause aligns with their values, or worse, when the leader usurping power belongs to their faction.

This fundamental misunderstanding, that dangerous precedents become acceptable when deployed for the "right" purposes or by the "right" people, is just as deadly to freedom, if not more so.

Dickinson drew on the Roman historian Sallust, who wrote in his account of a Senate speech by Julius Caesar, that bad precedents often start with good intentions.

"All bad precedents have originated in cases which were good; but when the control of the government falls into the hands of men who are incompetent or bad, your new precedent is transferred from those who well deserve and merit such punishment to the undeserving and blameless."

Thomas Gordon preserved Caesar's warning with full force in his translation of Sallust, highlighting the Thirty Tyrants of Athens: an example his audience would have recognized immediately.

"The Lacedaemonians, when they had subdued the Athenians, subjected that State to Thirty Governors. These began their Power, by executing, without Conviction, whomsoever they found notoriously wicked and obnoxious to all Men."

The people celebrated these initial executions. Finally, justice would be handed out to the corrupt. But celebration quickly became terror.

"Thenceforward, when, by degrees, they had strengthened their lawless Authority, they doomed to Death both Good and Bad, without Distinction; and thus held under Dread the whole Community. Such was the terrible Penalty, which these People, oppressed by Tyranny, paid for their ridiculous Joy."

Even Machiavelli, never known for squeamishness about power, recognized this danger in the ancient republics.

"Now in a well-ordered republic it should never be necessary to resort to extra-constitutional measures; for although they may for the time be beneficial, yet the precedent is pernicious..."

The reason, as Machiavelli explained, is inevitable abuse.

"...for if the practice is once established of disregarding the laws for good objects, they will in a little while be disregarded under that pretext for evil purposes."

John Locke took this warning to its logical conclusion. He argued that popular rulers who use unconstitutional power pose the greatest threat to liberty.

"That the reigns of good princes have been always most dangerous to the liberties of their people: for when their successors, managing the government with different thoughts, would draw the actions of those good rulers into precedent and make them the standard of their prerogative, as if what had been done only for the good of the people was a right in them to do, for the harm of the people."

FATAL ERROR

As Dickinson noted - because precedents often start small, the people generally don't take action against them until they have grown to a level where the pain is obvious.

"Indeed nations, in general, are not apt to think until they feel; and therefore nations in general have lost their liberty: For as violations of the rights of the governed, are commonly not only specious, but small at the beginning, they spread over the multitude in such a manner, as to touch individuals but slightly. Thus they are disregarded."

Drawing on his favorite biography of Cicero, Dickinson left us with the harsh reality: because small precedents look harmless to most, the "good" people get complacent, while the enemies of freedom keep pushing on.

"The republic is attacked always with greater vigor, than it is defended."

Understanding this history, Dickinson knew that the smaller the violation, the deadlier it becomes – because few people bother to fight it. Writing about the Townshend Acts, he exposed what most people missed – and why it mattered.

"Some persons may think this act of no consequence, because the duties are so small."

Then he delivered the blow.

"A fatal error."

Why fatal? Because the size of the violation wasn't the point – the precedent was. And the smaller the precedent, the more dangerous it actually is.

"That is the very circumstance most alarming to me. For I am convinced, that the authors of this law would never have obtained an act to raise so trifling a sum as it must do, had they not intended by it to establish a precedent for future use."

He closed with this perfect metaphor: IT'S A TRAP!

"To console ourselves with the smallness of the duties, is to walk deliberately into the snare that is set for us, praising the neatness of the workmanship."

While understanding and recognizing the trap is an essential step on the path to liberty, James Madison invoked an ancient phrase to remind us of the next.

"Let them exert the same wisdom, in watching agst. every evil lurking under plausible disguises, and growing up from small beginnings. Obsta principiis."

Chapter 7

THE ANCIENT MAXIM

"Like a cancer."

America was built on the understanding that constitutional violations are a deadly disease.

Give government an inch - and they will take a few thousand miles, and never stop. And before too long, it becomes a place where it's no longer a Republic, but a long slow coup. Or, as the Declaration of Independence put it, eating *"out our substance."*

Our rights. Our money. And everything in between.

The solution? The ancient Roman principle behind the American Revolution.

THE DISEASE

The Revolution was built on a hard truth: If the people allow even the smallest usurpation of power, that sets the stage for the deadly disease of total tyranny. As John Adams wrote, it gets worse over time.

"The nature of the encroachment upon [the] American constitution is such, as to grow every day more and more encroaching. Like a cancer, it eats faster and faster every hour."

John Dickinson addressed those who claimed that "now is not the time" to take a stand, whether they believed the usurpation was too small, or their ability to stop it too weak.

"Are these men ignorant, that usurpations, which might have been successfully opposed at first, acquire strength by continuance, and thus become irresistible?"

This mentality feeds the deadly cycle. Adams explained exactly how government uses it to bring the people to their knees.

"The revenue creates pensioners, and the pensioners urge for more revenue."

He wasn't talking about retirement plans. "Pensioners" meant anyone financially dependent on the government. He warned that as this dependent class grows, society devolves into corruption.

"The people grow less steady, spirited, and virtuous, the seekers more numerous and more corrupt, and every day increases the circles of their dependents and expectants, until virtue, integrity, public spirit, simplicity, and frugality, become the objects of ridicule and scorn, and vanity, luxury, foppery, selfishness, meanness, and downright venality swallow up the whole society."

OBSTA PRINCIPIIS

James Madison knew the United States wouldn't even exist if the people hadn't spotted the massive danger hidden inside a small tax on tea.

"The people of the U. S. owe their Independence & their liberty, to the wisdom of descrying in the minute tax of 3 pence on tea, the magnitude of the evil comprized in the precedent."

He warned Americans to keep using that wisdom, invoking a maxim thousands of years old.

"Let them exert the same wisdom, in watching agst. every evil lurking under plausible disguises, and growing up from small beginnings. Obsta principiis."

John Adams defined it in plain English.

"Obsta principiis - Nip the shoots of arbitrary power in the bud, is the only maxim which can ever preserve the liberties of any people"

That maxim comes from the Roman poet Ovid around 2 AD. It means you must stop the disease at the very start. If you wait, even the right cure could arrive too late.

"Resist beginnings; too late is the medicine prepared, when the disease has gained strength by long delay."

As Machiavelli documented, long before Claudius's quote about precedent creating precedent, this principle was a common understanding in the Roman Republic.

"Thus in all these cases the Romans did what all wise princes ought to do; namely, not only to look to all present troubles, but also to those of the future, against which they provided with the utmost prudence."

Drawing on the maxim that Ovid would later write, he noted they looked far in the future for potential dangers.

"For it is by foreseeing difficulties from afar that they are easily provided against; but awaiting their near approach, remedies are no longer in time, for the malady has become incurable."

Machiavelli also compared that danger to a deadly disease.

"It happens in such cases, as the doctors say of consumption, that in the early stages it is easy to cure, but difficult to recognize; whilst in the course of time, the disease not having been recognized and

cured in the beginning, it becomes easy to know, but difficult to cure."

He saw the exact same principle at work in the body politic. Resist the beginnings, or the Republic could be doomed.

"And thus it is in the affairs of state; for when the evils that arise in it are seen far ahead, which it is given only to a wise prince to do, then they are easily remedied; but when, in consequence of not having been foreseen, these evils are allowed to grow and assume such proportions that they become manifest to every one, then they can no longer be remedied."

ASLEEP

Given this history, it's no surprise that this phrase from Montesquieu was foundational for the American Revolution.

"Slavery is ever preceded by sleep."

He knew the opposite was also true. A tireless, eternally watchful people are the only ones capable of preserving freedom.

"But a people who find no rest in any situation, who continually explore every part, and feel nothing but pain, can hardly be lulled to sleep."

During the Revolution, Jonathan Mayhew took that ancient warning to the pulpit. Using a well-known biblical parable, he warned his congregation exactly what happens when the people fall asleep on their watch.

"For in the states and kingdoms of this world, it happens as it does in the field or church, according to the well-known parable, to this purpose; That while men sleep, then the enemy cometh and soweth tares, which cannot be rooted out again till the end of the world, without rooting out the wheat with them."

In his famous sermon, *The Snare Broken,* Mayhew grounded this in the timeless maxim that power always seeks to grow, and it always succeeds when left unchecked.

"Power aims at extending itself, and operating according to mere will, where-ever it meets with no ballance, check, controul or opposition of any kind."

He preached that preserving liberty means spotting every violation of it - and taking action to stop it.

"For which reason it will always be necessary, as was said before, for those who would preserve and perpetuate their liberties, to guard them with a wakeful attention; and in all righteous, just and prudent ways, to oppose the first encroachments on them. "Obsta principiis." After a while it will be too late."

John Dickinson reissued the same warning: stay on constant watch, or else.

"Indeed we ought firmly to believe, what is an undoubted truth, confirmed by the unhappy experience of many states heretofore free, that UNLESS THE MOST WATCHFUL ATTENTION BE EXERTED, A NEW SERVITUDE MAY BE SLIPPED UPON US, UNDER THE SANCTION OF USUAL AND RESPECTABLE TERMS."

John Adams connected all the dots. In order to stay free, the people must be awake, recognize even the smallest precedents, and follow the ancient maxim: oppose every advance, always.

"The spirit of liberty, is and ought to be a jealous, a watchful spirit. Obsta Principiis is her motto and maxim; knowing that her enemies are secret and cunning, making the earliest advances slowly, silently and softly, and that according to her unerring oracle Tacitus, "the first advances of tyranny are steep and perilous, but when once you are entered, parties and instruments are ready to espouse you."

THE DEFAULT

To prevent such precedent from gaining a foothold, Dickinson said the best approach for a free people - against even the smallest steps - is to stay vigilant: awake, aware, and active.

"A FREE people therefore can never be too quick in observing, nor too firm in opposing the beginnings of alteration either in form or reality, respecting institutions formed for their security."

He summed up this view by quoting the Roman satirist Persius to sign off the ninth of his *Letters from a Farmer in Pennsylvania*.

"Oppose a disease at its beginning."

They all knew opposing a disease required more than words. But being successful in action started with a strong moral foundation of exactly where loyalties lie.

Chapter 8

TRUE LOYALTY

"It is a very great mistake to imagine that the Object of Loyalty is the Authority and Interest of one individual Man."

Decades before the Declaration of Independence, Samuel Adams understood the foundation of what became the American Revolution. It was a complete rejection of the ancient mode of humanity: total allegiance to a person, or even a group of people.

But those in power have played the same trick for centuries: they flip the script. They make criminals out of anyone who stands on principle, and saints out of those who bow to tyranny.

Adams saw this deception clearly. He knew exactly how tyrants use language to enslave people, how they twist words like "loyalty" and "sedition" into weapons against liberty itself.

THE DEFINITION

Before we can define true loyalty, we have to start at the source of all political manipulation - language. In 1748, a 26-year-old

Samuel Adams opened his essay on *Loyalty and Sedition* by exposing how those in power corrupt language itself.

"Perhaps no Words have been more misunderstood or perverted, than the Words Loyalty and Sedition."

To clear any confusion, Adams defined loyalty by tying it directly to the Constitution

"The former I take to signify a firm and inviolable attachment to a legal Constitution."

With moral duty as his foundation, Adams laid out exactly what this attachment requires: the people must know the Constitution thoroughly, defend it relentlessly, and be ready to support laws that preserve it.

"True Loyalty in the Sense just now Explain'd ... includes in it a thorough Knowledge of our Constitution, its Inconveniences and Defects, as well as its real Advantages; a becoming Jealousy of our Immunities, and a steadfast Resolution to maintain them. A habitual Readiness to support and strengthen the Execution of those Laws which flow from the Constitution, and tend to preserve it."

Adams drew this definition from other writers such as Thomas Gordon. He anchored loyalty to law and constitutional government.

"In an honest sense, indeed in common sense, it means no more than the squaring our actions by the rules of good laws, and an attachment to a constitution supported by such."

For Adams, real loyalty could not exist under a government that ignores the constitution and wields arbitrary power.

"It cannot indeed subsist in an arbitrary Government, because it is founded in the Love and Possession of Liberty."

SEDITION

Adams then turned to sedition, describing it as a deadly disease.

"But Sedition is founded on the deprav'd and inordinate Passions of the Mind: It is a weak, feverish, sickly thing, a boisterous and unnatural Vigour, which cannot support it self long, and oftentimes destroys the unhappy Patient."

Building on this, Adams defined sedition as any attempt to destroy the constitution.

"The latter, all Tendencies, Machinations, and Attempts to overset a legal Constitution."

He made the principle concrete. Restricting liberty or wielding power outside the constitution is disloyalty, bordering on treason.

"But as the Love of Liberty is the very Soul of Loyalty, and the Lust of Preeminence and Money the Main Spring of Sedition, so all Attempts to curtail and destroy our Liberties, or to introduce selfish and arbitrary Measures, are equally a Deviation from true Loyalty, and an Approach to Sedition."

THE REAL REBELS

Adams left no room for compromise. He didn't limit disloyalty to those actively breaking the constitution. Merely **suggesting** violations of the constitution, or **tolerating** any such attempts, means you're disloyal.

"Whosoever therefore insinuates Notions of Government contrary to the Constitution or in any degree winks at any Measures to suppress or even to weaken it is not a loyal Man."

Adams then went even further. Those who actively work to defend and spread unconstitutional power are the worst offenders.

"He that leaves no Stone unturn'd to defend and propagate the Schemes of illegal Power, cannot be esteem'd a Loyal Man."

Thomas Gordon delivered the hard truth. People who wield power outside the constitution are not just misguided: they are the real enemies.

"Every lawless prince is a rebel."

Gordon didn't just limit this to people in government. The people who obey a rebel are rebels right along with him.

"To obey one who obeys no law, is a departure from all loyalty, and an outrage committed upon it; and that both he who commands, and he who obeys, are outlaws and disloyalists."

THE TACTIC

Tyrants never lack willing tools ready to cheerlead their every move. Gordon exposed this as a deliberate strategy used throughout history.

"Whoever is lawless, is disloyal; and to boast of loyalty to disloyalty, is strange nonsense; a paradox first invented by solemn and pernicious pedants, whose trade it is to pervert the use of words and the meaning of things, to abuse and confound the human understanding, and to mislead the world into misery and darkness."

Samuel Adams understood the tactic: Those who seek to expand unconstitutional power flip the meaning of words upside down.

"But we oftentimes perceive such Signification assum'd by those who find the wrong Use of these Words conducive to the Support and Increase of Power and Gain, that it is difficult to tell whether Loyalty be really commendable, or Sedition blameworthy."

The result? As Gordon explained, the guilty are celebrated, and the righteous are condemned.

"In short, that all the instruments and partners of his crying crimes are loyalists; and all who defend law, virtue, and mankind, against such monsters, are rebels, and assuredly damned, for preventing or resisting actions which deserve damnation."

Gordon understood this perversion of language as deliberate manipulation. The goal is to make loyalty entirely about the person in power. Support the leader, and you are celebrated. Oppose him, and you are condemned.

"It is indeed a trick, more than a mistake; I mean of those who would assert or rather create a sort of loyalty to ministers, and make every thing which they do not like an offence against their master."

Algernon Sidney understood the irony. Those demanding blind loyalty to one man not only turn him into a monster, they also put him in grave danger.

"Those who boast of their loyalty, and think they give testimonies of it, when they addict themselves to the will of one man, tho contrary to the law from whence that quality is derived, may consider, that by putting their masters upon illegal courses they certainly make them the worst of men, and bring them into danger of being also the most miserable."

For Samuel Adams, it all came down to one key point. Loyalty to a person rather than to the constitution and liberty? He condemned that as a fatal error.

"It is a very great mistake to imagine that the Object of Loyalty is the Authority and Interest of one individual Man, however dignified by the Applause or enriched by the Success of Popular Actions."

He warned that the tragic result of this mistake is etched in the pages of history.

"This has led Millions into such a degree of Dependance and Submission that they have at length found themselves oblig'd to

homage the Instruments of their Ruin, at the very Time they were at Work to effect it."

This understanding was an essential part of the backbone of the American Revolution. The inverse is also true: a people truly loyal to their constitution and their liberty will always find the courage to protect them both.

Chapter 9

NONCOMPLIANCE

"Americans cannot submit."

The Revolution was built on the understanding that compliance with arbitrary power isn't safety or peace.

It's surrender.

This is an essential, but long-forgotten foundation of American independence: laws made outside the limits of the constitution are not law at all.

And they should be treated that way too.

DISOBEY

The starting point? Government doesn't get to do whatever it wants. It has limits.

As future third Chief Justice Oliver Ellsworth put it, when it goes beyond those limits, those acts aren't law. They are void right from the start.

"If they make a law which the Constitution does not authorize, it is void."

Declaring something void is one thing. But making it that way in practice is another. And that starts with a refusal to comply with arbitrary power.

In his Virginia Resolves against the Stamp Act, Patrick Henry declared that when government exceeds its limits, the people are not required to obey.

"The Inhabitants of this Colony, are not bound to yield Obedience to any Law or Ordinance whatever, designed to impose any Taxation whatsoever upon them, other than the Laws or Ordinances of the General Assembly aforesaid."

In the Suffolk Resolves against the Coercive Acts, Joseph Warren took the same position, writing that *"no Obedience is due"* to those acts, and they *"may be rejected as the Attempts of a wicked Administration to enslave America."*

This view was widely held throughout the Revolution. But the British persisted in passing more arbitrary acts. Their goal, as John Dickinson wrote, was to assert the power of Parliament and gain the obedience of the colonies.

"No man, who considers the conduct of the parliament since the repeal of the Stamp Act, and the disposition of many people at home, can doubt, that the chief object of attention there, is, to use Mr. Greenville's expression, 'providing that the DEPENDENCE and OBEDIENCE of the colonies be asserted and maintained.'"

Despite this, by the time the First Continental Congress met in 1774, noncompliance was the American default. Obedience to arbitrary power was not even on the table.

"To these grievous acts and measures Americans cannot submit."

FOUNDATION

Ellsworth's view that laws beyond the limits of the Constitution are void wasn't new or radical when he made the statement in 1788. It went right back to the heart of the Revolution in 1761, specifically James Otis Jr.'s speech against the writs of assistance.

"An Act against the constitution is void."

Even under the unwritten British constitution, this explained the difference between free people and subjects.

John Jay gave us the true hierarchy: the Creator, then the people, and government at the very bottom.

"You and all men were created free, and authorized to establish civil government, for the preservation of your rights against oppression, and the security of that freedom which God hath given you, against the rapacious hand of tyranny and lawless power."

For Alexander Hamilton, the logical result of this hierarchy is that government is based on consent, and has limits beyond which it is not authorized to go.

"Hence also, the origin of all civil government, justly established, must be a voluntary compact, between the rulers and the ruled; and must be liable to such limitations, as are necessary for the security of the absolute rights of the latter."

Anything beyond those limits? That is usurpation. It is stolen power, and no one has a moral or legal obligation to obey a thief.

"To grasp at a more extensive power than they are willing to entrust, is to violate that law of nature, which gives every man a right to his personal liberty; and can, therefore, confer no obligation to obedience."

Government, then, exists to act as an agent of the people. It is the hired help. So the people themselves, John Dickinson wrote, get to decide when government goes too far.

"They will always have the same rights, that all free states have, of judging when their privileges are invaded, and of using all prudent measures for preserving them."

Thomas Jefferson put that in practice in 1774 in response to a long list of British acts going back over a century. But first, he started with an important caveat: an act is not null and void merely because of its policy results.

"We do not point out to his majesty the injustice of these acts, with intent to rest on that principle the cause of their nullity."

Instead, it is based on something much deeper: whether or not an act stays within the bounds of a constitution.

"The true ground on which we declare these acts void is, that the British parliament has no right to exercise authority over us."

To reject this hierarchy - as James Madison later wrote - is to reject the Declaration of Independence.

"A plain denial of the fundamental principle on which our independence itself was declared."

LINEAGE

At its core, the Revolution was built on the idea that breaking laws, in and of itself, is not inherently wrong. The Union was founded by people refusing to comply with a whole host of British acts.

They didn't invent this principle. It was deeply rooted in their history and tradition.

For example, Josiah Quincy, in an essay opposing the Boston Port Bill, paraphrased a well-known medieval Catalan-Aragonese oath of allegiance to the King of Aragon. He did this to prove that allegiance and obedience have very clear limits.

"We, who are each of us as good, and who are altogether more powerful than you, promise obedience to your government, IF YOU MAINTAIN OUR RIGHTS AND LIBERTIES; IF NOT, NOT."

John Locke's *Two Treatises*, written 75 years before the Stamp Act, provided the intellectual foundation for Patrick Henry's position that the people are not bound to obey unconstitutional power.

"Whenever the legislators endeavour to take away, and destroy the property of the people, or to reduce them to slavery under arbitrary power, they put themselves into a state of war with the people, who are thereupon absolved from any farther obedience."

Algernon Sidney took the next step, arguing that noncompliance was more than just an option - it was essential.

"That which is not just, is not Law; and that which is not Law, ought not to be obeyed."

Hugo Grotius had previously connected this to natural rights.

"This is allowed by all good Men, that if the civil Powers command any Thing contrary to the Law of Nature, or the Commands of God, they are not to be obeyed."

But this principle goes back even further. Centuries earlier, Thomas Aquinas laid out the framework for how to respond to abuses of power.

The starting point? When government exceeds its legal limits, the people have no **obligation** to obey, and they retain the **choice** to refuse.

"In this case the subject is not obliged to obey, but neither is he obliged not to obey."

However, he warned, some abuses demand a much higher moral duty.

"A commandment emanating from the authority might be contrary to the very end in view of which authority is instituted."

In that case, the people are not just absolved from obedience. They have a positive **duty** to disobey.

"We not only are not obliged to obey but we are also obliged not to obey, according to the example of the holy martyrs who preferred death to obeying those ungodly tyrants."

CHAINS

Whether an act of arbitrary power rises to that level or not, John Dickinson warned that compliance with unconstitutional acts, like the Stamp Act, is dangerous because it guarantees tyranny.

"If you comply with the Act by using Stamped Papers, you fix, you rivet perpetual Chains upon your unhappy Country."

He knew every time a people allow the enforcement of one unconstitutional act, they establish the precedent for more of the same in the future.

"You unnecessarily, voluntarily establish the detestable Precedent, which those who have forged your Fetters ardently wish for, to varnish the future Exercise of this new claimed Authority."

This echoed Sidney's warning from almost a century earlier: submission doesn't buy peace or safety; it guarantees destruction.

"People must certainly perish, who tamely suffer themselves to be oppress'd ... by the injustice, cruelty and malice of an ill magistrate."

From this, Dickinson viewed every unconstitutional act as a test of the people's backbone and resolve of the people.

"If you quietly bend your Necks to that Yoke, you prove yourselves ready to receive any Bondage to which your Lords and Masters shall please to subject you."

In Pennsylvania, Benjamin Rush made the cost of compliance with the tax on tea explicit. Let the tea come ashore, and the cause of liberty was lost - permanently.

"Should it be landed, it is to be feared it will find its way amongst us. Then farewell American liberty. We are undone forever."

Like Dickinson and the broader opposition to the Stamp Act in 1765, the fight in 1773 wasn't over tea, or even the tax itself. It was over whether Americans would accept the chains that always accompany compliance with arbitrary power.

LATER

Despite this, there are always those who claim 'now is not the time' to disobey or resist. Samuel Adams rejected that outright, warning the "wait till later" approach just guarantees the destruction of liberty.

"If the liberties of America are ever compleatly ruined, of which in my opinion there is now the utmost danger, it will in all probability be the consequence of a mistaken notion of prudence, which leads men to acquiesce in measures of the most destructive tendency for the sake of present ease."

Otis called these people, the ones begging for delay, the greatest threat to liberty.

"There is however no character so dangerous to liberty as the man of prudence. You may possibly be right, but at this juncture it is not prudent to insist upon it, is the language of artful courtiers, and has done more hurt than can well be imagined."

His sister, Mercy Otis Warren, recognized this as a fatal flaw in human nature throughout history. The people fall asleep on their watch because they believe doing the right thing is too dangerous or requires too much effort.

"There is a certain supineness which generally overspreads the multitude, and disposes mankind to submit quietly to any form of government, rather than to be at the expense and hazard of resistance."

As a result, they become trapped in a cycle of obedience, no matter how tyrannical the laws become.

"They become attached to ancient modes by habits of obedience, though the reins of authority are sometimes held by the most rigorous hand."

The historical result of this apathy is absolutely brutal.

"Thus we have seen in all ages the many become the slaves of the few; preferring the wretched tranquility of inglorious ease, they patiently yield to despotic masters."

But even the most submissive people have a breaking point. Sometimes they find their backbone only after enduring *"a long train of abuses and usurpations."*

"Until awakened by multiplied wrongs to the feelings of human nature; which when once aroused to a consciousness of the native freedom and equal rights of man, every revolts at the idea of servitude."

While this certainly leaves a glimmer of hope, John Adams warned that the longer the people wait, the more difficult and dangerous the remedy becomes.

"It is one of these early advances, these first approaches of arbitrary power, which are the most dangerous of all, and if not prevented,

but suffered to steal into precedents, will leave no hope of a remedy without recourse to nature, violence, and war."

BACKBONE

Rather than endlessly waiting, James Otis Jr. held that later is always the wrong time, and now is always the right time.

"When our rights are invaded, it is high time to throw aside prudence."

Joseph Hawley warned of the inevitable consequence: a people who do not defend their rights are guaranteed to lose them.

"The people or state who will not or cannot defend their liberties and rights will not have any for any long time."

Otis took it even further. Those demanding endless, blind obedience are traitors.

"He that would palm the doctrine of unlimited passive obedience and non-resistance upon mankind ...is not only a fool and a knave, but a rebel against common sense, as well as the laws of God, of Nature, and his Country."

This "harmonizing sentiment" of the day was so prominent that John Adams later recalled how he was raised with it.

"Certainly I was bred in the deepest contempt and abhorrence of the doctrines of Passive Obedience, and Non-resistance."

Otis argued this must be the default American position. Every violation of rights, no matter how small, demands an immediate response.

"It is my countrymen of the utmost consequence that we boldly oppose the least infraction of our charter, and rights as men. Obsta Principiis is a maxim never to be forgot: If we do not resist at the first attack, it may soon be too late."

But that still left a major question wide open. At what point does arbitrary power become so abusive that the duty of resistance moves from peaceful noncompliance to more active measures?

Chapter 10

RESIST

"W*e fear not death."*

For John Hancock and the American Revolutionaries, "Liberty or Death" wasn't just a slogan.

It was a warning.

Rights are not gifts from government. Pass laws that violate them, and we will not comply.

Persist, and we will resist. And you will pay the price.

This natural rights foundation was built on a two-thousand year lineage that made *"Rebellion to tyrants"* not just a suggestion, but a moral duty: *"Obedience to God."*

NEXT STEP

The Declaration of Independence famously connected this view of rebellion as duty.

"When a long train of abuses and usurpations, pursuing invariably the same Object evinces a design to reduce them under absolute

Despotism, it is their right, it is their duty, to throw off such Government, and to provide new Guards for their future security."

To understand when resistance rises to the level of duty, we must start at the foundational principle. Thomas Gordon warned in *Cato's Letters* that tyranny thrives on passive compliance.

"That not to resist any man's wickedness, is to encourage it."

The Founders and Old Revolutionaries understood this well, seeing noncompliance with unconstitutional acts as an essential strategic option that could also rise to the level of duty.

There are times, however, when tyrants persist and noncompliance is no longer enough. At that point, a far more active defense of liberty becomes not just a right, but a duty.

But, as the Declaration of Independence made clear, that becomes morally justified only after a long, patient process.

In it, the Second Continental Congress declared that the very purpose of government is to protect the natural rights *"life, liberty, and the pursuit of happiness."*

When government fails in that duty, or actively destroys those rights, the people have a remedy.

"Whenever any Form of Government becomes destructive of these ends, it is the Right of the People to alter or to abolish it, and to institute new Government, laying its foundation on such principles and organizing its powers in such form, as to them shall seem most likely to effect their Safety and Happiness."

But this did not mean the people could jump from a single act of arbitrary power directly to armed revolt.

"Prudence, indeed, will dictate that Governments long established should not be changed for light and transient causes."

Aristotle argued in 350 BC that even when things rise to that level, the people who **should** do something usually don't.

"Those who excel in virtue have the best right of all to rebel (for they alone can with reason be deemed absolutely unequal), but then they are of all men the least inclined to do so."

This historical truth was also reflected in the Declaration.

"And accordingly all experience hath shewn, that mankind are more disposed to suffer, while evils are sufferable, than to right themselves by abolishing the forms to which they are accustomed."

Jefferson and company were clear that the present suffering in 1776 America wasn't due to weakness. It was patience.

"Such has been the patient sufferance of these Colonies; and such is now the necessity which constrains them to alter their former Systems of Government."

Eventually, the threshold was crossed, and stopping tyranny rose to the level of duty.

"When a long train of abuses and usurpations, pursuing invariably the same Object evinces a design to reduce them under absolute Despotism, it is their right, it is their duty, to throw off such Government, and to provide new Guards for their future security."

PATIENT PROCESS

This famous "expression of the American mind" was built on the hierarchy of power underlying the Revolution: Creator, then the people, with government at the bottom.

This means the ultimate, sovereign power to determine when government goes too far rests with the people themselves. John Allen connected this with the natural right of self-defense.

"Though you cannot prevent the unconstitutional design of the arbitrary power of the British ministry; yet you have an undoubted right to resist and prevent their reigning over you; or ruining you in the Violation of your laws and rights."

However, as to when that line is crossed into "reigning" or "ruining" - there was no clear **legal** answer. It was, as John Dickinson put it, a gray area.

"No English lawyer, as we remember, has pointed out precisely the line beyond which, if a king, shall "go," resistance becomes lawful."

Despite lacking a clearly drawn line, Dickinson insisted one indeed existed.

"We assert, a line there must be, and shall now proceed with great deference to the judgment of others, to trace that line, according to the ideas we entertain."

In his widely-read sermon to the "Ancient and Honorable Artillery-Company, in Boston," Rev. Simeon Howard provided the religious and philosophical justification for physically defending liberty against *"external force and constraint."* He made one of the best efforts to clarify exactly when that line is crossed.

As Samuel Adams did the prior year, Howard recognized that the right of self-defense, arising from the duty of self-preservation, dictated that the strategy must fit the situation.

"Now for men to stand fast in their liberty means, in general, resisting the attempts that are made against it, in the best and most effectual manner they can."

That resistance could take many forms, like peaceful noncompliance. Howard explained the American view: hold the line with nonviolent actions before taking more active measures.

"When any one's liberty is attacked or threatened, he is first to try gentle methods for his safety; to reason with, and persuade the

adversary to desist, if there be opportunity for it; or get out of his way, if he can; and if by such means he can prevent the injury, he is to use no other."

Arthur Lee of Virginia made the same case. The revolutionaries felt a moral duty to try every peaceful method possible before resorting to force.

"Yet they are too much enlightened not to know, that they cannot be justified in proceeding to extremities, till they have tried every means of obtaining redress in vain."

Lee pointed out the same truth later included in the Declaration of Independence: Americans dealt with this patiently and peacefully for years.

"The Americans have in fact exhausted every peaceable means of ob|taining redress. for seven years they have incessantly complained and petitioned for redress; their return has invariably been a repetition of injuries, aggravated by the most intolerable insults. There has not been a single instance in which they have complained, without being rebuked, or in which they have been complained against, without being punished."

Although they emphasized that the first steps must be nonviolent, Howard summed up the historical truth: even if those actions succeed temporarily, the worst tyrants keep coming back for more.

"But the experience of all ages has shewn, that those, who are so unreasonable as to form designs of injuring others, are seldom to be diverted from their purpose by argument and persuasion alone: Notwithstanding all that can be said to shew the injustice and inhumanity of their attempt, they persist in it, till they have gratified the unruly passion which set them to work."

In that scenario, patience that seems to last forever isn't really patience. It's surrender.

"And in this case, what is to be done by the sufferer? Is he to use no other means for his safety, but remonstrance or flight, when these will not secure him? Is he patiently to take the injury and suffer himself to be robbed of his liberty or his life, if the adversary sees fit to take it? Nature certainly forbids this tame submission, and loudly calls to a more vigorous defence."

This wasn't just theory. John Dickinson pointed to their own well-known history and tradition of armed resistance.

"If at length it becomes undoubted, that an inveterate resolution is formed to annihilate the liberties of the governed, the English history affords frequent examples of resistance by force."

For Dickinson, while that breaking point was not clearly delineated, the ultimate decision rested with the people themselves.

"What particular circumstances will in any future case justify such resistance, can never be ascertained till they happen. Perhaps it may be allowable to say, generally, that it never can be justifiable, until the people are FULLY CONVINCED, that any further submission will be destructive to their happiness."

SELF PRESERVATION

As Dickinson and Thomas Jefferson explained in the *Declaration of the Causes and Necessity of Taking up Arms*, the "more vigorous defense" that began at the battles of Lexington and Concord was "*against Violence actually offered*," and it followed the defensive escalation that Howard advised - to the letter.

"Self-preservation is one of the strongest, and a universal principle of the human mind: And this principle allows of every thing necessary to self-defence, opposing force to force, and violence to violence. This is so universally allowed that I need not attempt to prove it."

In his widely-read sermon "concerning unlimited submission and non-resistance to the higher powers," Rev. Jonathan Mayhew preached that the people's right of self-defense was a gift from their Creator. Therefore, it was not radical to use it to protect their rights.

"For a nation thus abused to arise unanimously, and to resist their prince, even to the dethroning him, is not criminal; but a reasonable way of vindicating their liberties and just rights; it is making use of the means, and the only means, which God has put into their power, for mutual and self-defence."

Taking it a step further, he argued that there is a point where tyranny becomes so abusive that it is morally criminal **not** to resist.

"And it would be highly criminal in them, not to make use of this means. It would be stupid tameness, and unaccountable folly, for whole nations to suffer one unreasonable, ambitious and cruel man, to wanton and riot in their misery. And in such a case it would, of the two, be more rational to suppose, that they that did NOT resist, than that they who did, would receive to themselves damnation."

Samuel Adams took that position to its logical conclusion. There is nothing worse than an attack on the rights of the people, or a failure to defend them against all enemies, foreign or domestic.

"The people hold the Invasion of their Rights & Liberties the most horrid rebellion and a Neglect to defend them against any Power whatsoever the highest Treason."

Almost four years before the war, Adams clearly articulated the hard line that built American independence. When power is arbitrary, lawless, and unconstitutional, resistance is not just optional.

It's a moral imperative - a duty.

"Who will presume to say that the people have not a right, or that it is not their indispensible duty to God and their Country, by all rational means in their power to RESIST THEM."

There are always those who fearmonger. They warn of chaos and calamity if the people themselves resist government power in any form. But as Thomas Gordon put it, the truth is exactly the opposite.

"It is said, that the doctrine of resistance would destroy the peace of the world: But it may be more truly said, that the contrary doctrine would destroy the world itself, as it has already some of the best countries in it."

Quoting Cato the Younger through the Roman historian Sallust, Benjamin Franklin reminded us that this defense has to be supported by courage.

"Be not deceived; Divine assistance and protection are not to be obtained by timorous prayers and. To succeed, you must join salutary counsels, vigilance, and courageous actions."

In the end, Thomas Paine was right. Freedom isn't going to defend itself. It never did, and it never will.

"Those who expect to reap the blessings of freedom, must, like men, undergo the fatigues of supporting it."

THE PRICE

Making a declaration is one thing. As Jefferson later wrote, it takes backbone to make it stick.

"We are not to expect to be translated from despotism to liberty, in a feather-bed."

Few explained better than Dickinson how well the founders and old revolutionaries understood the costs of protecting and defending their rights.

"They are born with us; exist with us; and cannot be taken from us by any human power, without taking our lives."

But as John Hancock put it, that wasn't something to fear. He called out those who valued their skin more than liberty as unmanly cowards.

"Death is the creature of a Poltroon's brains; 'tis immortality, to sacrifice our|selves for the salvation of our country. We fear not death."

The famous phrase "give me liberty or give me death" was no isolated sentiment. A litany of similar perspectives appeared in speeches, essays, and letters throughout the Revolution, with this from Joseph Warren being one of the most powerful.

"Vigilance, activity, and patience are necessary at this time: but the mistress we court is LIBERTY; and it is better to die than not to obtain her."

This was not limited to the courage of patriots and their willingness to sacrifice. As George Washington wrote, it was also a promise of consequences for tyrants.

"I hope that every diabolical attempt to deprive Mankind of their Inherent Rights and Priviledges, whether made in the East—West—North—or South, will be attended with disappointment and disgrace; and that the Authors—in the end—will be brought to such punishment as an injured People have a right to Inflict."

And it wasn't just tough talk either. When they said liberty or death - they meant it.

On July 6, 1775 - just weeks after the battles of Lexington and Concord, and the "shot heard 'round the world" - the Second Continental Congress unanimously passed the Declaration of the Causes and Necessity of Taking up Arms. In it, Thomas Jefferson and John Dickinson made it clear to the world that they were fighting to defend their natural rights.

"In our own native Land, in defence of the Freedom that is our Birthright, and which we ever enjoyed till the late Violation of it—for the protection of our Property, acquired solely by the honest Industry of our fore-fathers and ourselves, against Violence actually offered, we have taken up Arms. We shall lay them down when Hostilities shall cease on the part of the Aggressors, and all danger of their being renewed shall be removed, and not before."

DUTY

It is not easy to find that kind of courage. But the American revolutionaries possessed an almost endless reservoir of it because they saw it as a moral imperative. Or as Samuel Adams put it, their duty.

"The liberties of our Country, the freedom of our civil constitution are worth defending at all hazards: And it is our duty to defend them against all attacks."

In December 1776, John Jay connected all the dots. First, the foundation: rights come from the Creator, and government is simply an agent existing to protect them.

"You and all men were created free, and authorized to establish civil government, for the preservation of your rights against oppression, and the security of that freedom which God hath given you, against the rapacious hand of tyranny and lawless power."

When the hired help crosses the line and becomes an enemy of freedom, it is not just a right, but a duty to stop them.

"It is, therefore not only necessary to the well-being of society, but the duty of every man, to oppose and repel all those, by whatever name or title distinguished, who prostitute the powers of government to destroy the happiness and freedom of the people over whom they may be appointed to rule."

So it should be no surprise that shortly after the Declaration of Independence was approved, Benjamin Franklin saw "liberty or death" as so vital to the American cause, a moral duty, that he recommended this version of it for the Great Seal of these United States.

"Rebellion to tyrants is obedience to God."

Chapter 11

THE BETRAYAL

Writing to Samuel Adams in 1787, Richard Henry Lee rejected the notion that *"the good people of the U. States in their late generous contest"* had any intention of rebuilding the system they fought a long, bloody war to secede from.

"They had no idea of being brought under despotic rule under the notion of 'Strong government,' or in form of elective despotism."

It did not matter if anyone could argue that such a system would be rich and prosperous, as empires have always been, at least temporarily.

"Chains being still Chains, whether made of gold or iron."

Unfortunately, that's exactly where things have gone for a long time.

The system we live under today is very much the same, in practice and effect, as the British system of the eighteenth century.

THE FINAL SAY

Prior to independence, Americans lived under a system where government was sovereign and held final authority. That same government gave itself power over the colonies in "all cases whatsoever."

As a result, government could and would do whatever it wanted until government changed its mind.

Compare that to the American system today: not how it is supposed to be under the Constitution, but how it plays out in practice.

This is exactly what John Dickinson, citing Corinthians, warned about.

"Nothing is more certain, than that the forms of liberty may be retained, when the substance is gone. In government, as well as in religion, 'The letter killeth, but the spirit giveth life.'"

The modern facade is far different from what operates underneath. It begins with the fact that Americans wholeheartedly support a bastardization of the constitutional system where government gets the final and ultimate say in determining if it is following its own rules.

This shows up most prominently through federal lawsuits.

Most people believe that when the federal government acts unconstitutionally, the best recourse is to file a lawsuit to stop it.

But the federal courts are part of the federal government.

Waiting on part of the federal government to tell the federal government to stop doing what the federal government wasn't supposed to do in the first place isn't what would happen in a real "land of the free."

A free people would claim their rights, *"as derived from the laws of nature"* and declare the act void, whether the government agrees with them, or not.

Instead, Americans today wait for government to decide for them. That's a population on its knees, begging for scraps.

On its own, this is a disaster.

But it gets worse when combined with the commonly held view of the Supremacy Clause: that federal law is always supreme until the federal government decides otherwise.

With that one-two punch of federal supremacy and final authority - there's not much difference from the British system under the Declaratory Act, where their law was supreme "in all cases whatsoever."

Until government decided to change course.

The only real difference in practice comes down to a handful of elections every few years. But Thomas Paine warned that simply choosing who wields power does not make a people free. The power itself is the problem.

"It is not because a part of the government is elective, that makes it less a despotism, if the persons so elected possess afterwards, as a parliament, unlimited powers. Election, in this case, becomes separated from representation, and the candidates are candidates for despotism."

ENEMIES WITHIN

The American Revolution was a historic shift: a "radical change" in the people themselves. To throw away that victory and return to the starting point where Americans live under the yoke of arbitrary power has taken something far more dangerous than all the acts of the British Parliament and the redcoats sent to enforce them.

But this surrender was no blind spot. We were warned that the most dangerous enemy would not come from across the ocean.

Writing in December 1778, before the war had even reached its bloody peak, Benjamin Rush recognized the greatest danger had already shifted away from the British government.

"The time is now past when the least danger is to be apprehended to our liberties from the power of Britain, the arts of commissioners, or the machinations of tories."

He was not talking about military battles. He was talking about the more important battles, and enemies, within.

"Tyranny can now enter our country only in the shape of a whig. All our jealousy should be of ourselves. All our fears should be of our great men, whether in civil or military authority."

Writing to William Gordon, he explained that freedom has a strict prerequisite.

"Virtue, virtue alone, my dear friend, is the basis of a republic."

To Rush and the revolutionaries, a truly virtuous people would never tolerate or submit to arbitrary power, because they viewed compliance with tyranny as a moral failure that leads directly to political slavery.

But even that prerequisite has a price. A people cannot claim and defend rights they do not recognize. Rush knew education is essential.

"Freedom can exist only in the society of knowledge. Without learning, men are incapable of knowing their rights."

He quoted Cesare Beccaria to expose what tyrants fear most: a people who know too much.

"When the clouds of ignorance are dispelled by the radiance of knowledge, authority trembles."

The enemies within have built their power on the ultimate one-two punch for tyranny: ignorance and moral decay.

Chapter 12

THE ONE TWO PUNCH

"It is in the Interest of Tyrants to reduce the People to Ignorance and Vice."

Observing the path to tyranny throughout history, Samuel Adams sounded almost prophetic in describing the one-two punch that has led to a complete betrayal of the principles of the American Revolution.

He knew that freedom is built on the opposite foundation.

"For they cannot live in any Country where Virtue and Knowledge prevail."

IGNORANCE

Thomas Jefferson understood what most people don't even consider today: Ignorance and freedom can never coexist.

"If a nation expects to be ignorant and free ... it expects what never was and never will be."

Thomas Paine saw this dynamic as a pattern across history.

Tyrants have always weaponized ignorance for one simple reason: educated people argue, while ignorant people obey.

"Reason and Ignorance, the opposites of each other, influence the great bulk of mankind. Reason obeys itself; and Ignorance submits to whatever is dictated to it."

In this view, Paine was channeling Montesquieu, who knew that ignorance leads people to "trust the experts" who gladly tell them what to do, even though they're often ignorant as well.

"Excessive obedience supposes ignorance in the person that obeys: the same it supposes in him that commands; for he has no occasion to deliberate, to doubt, to reason; he has only to will."

In the early 17th Century, Sir Francis Bacon exposed the excuse that rulers use to suppress real education. He noted they have always feared knowledge because they believe it breeds resistance to their power.

"It introduces a relaxation in government, as every man is more ready to argue than obey."

To show how deeply ingrained this view is, Bacon reached back even further to the ancients. He pointed to a well-known story from the Greco-Roman philosopher and biographer Plutarch. Cato the Elder saw a visiting Greek philosopher not as what he was - a diplomat - but as a threat to the regime, prompting him to convince the Roman Senate to expel him immediately.

"Whence Cato the censor - when Carneades came ambassador to Rome, and the young Romans, allured with his eloquence, flocked about him - gave counsel in open senate, to grant him his despatch immediately."

Why was Cato so eager to banish him? His fear wasn't that Carneades was wrong with his philosophy. It was that he made people think. And a thinking public just might not like their government.

"Lest he should infect the minds of the youth, and insensibly occasion an alteration in the State."

FORCED AND CONTROLLED

That was Ancient Rome. In 1765, John Adams wrote about what came after.

He examined over 1000 years of European history from the 5th century through the mid-16th century, identifying how tyranny maintained itself across the continent through forced ignorance.

"They have accordingly laboured, in all ages, to wrest from the populace, as they are contemptuously called, the knowledge of their rights and wrongs, and the power to assert the former or redress the latter."

The mechanism was a dual system of church and state control - specifically Canon and Feudal law, which Adams pointed out was implemented almost everywhere.

"Adopted by almost all the princes of Europe, and wrought into the constitutions of their government."

The result was **controlled** education: just enough knowledge to be a useful servant, not enough to rebel.

"In this manner, the common people were held together, in herds and clans, in a state of servile dependance on their lords; bound, even by the tenure of their lands to follow them, whenever they commanded, to their wars; and in a state of total ignorance of every thing divine and human, excepting the use of arms, and the culture of their lands."

But that kind of widespread, enforced ignorance couldn't last forever. As Adams noted, the dissemination of knowledge eventually broke through the system's grip.

"From the time of the reformation, to the first settlement of America, knowledge gradually spread in Europe, but especially in England; and in proportion as that increased and spread among the people, ecclesiastical and civil tyranny, which I use as synonimous expressions, for the cannon and feudal laws, seem to have lost their strength and weight."

WHACK A MOLE

The more people learned, the more tyrants had to adapt. So, as John Locke pointed out, they shifted to a propaganda-style approach - weaponizing language and twisting words to keep the truth hidden in plain sight.

"Thus learned ignorance, and this art of keeping, even inquisitive men, from true knowledge, hath been propagated in the world, and hath much perplexed whilst it pretended to inform the understanding."

And when all else fails? They'll just lie.

John Dickinson saw that exact pattern all through history.

"All artful rulers, who strive to extend their power beyond its just limits, endeavor to give to their attempts as much semblance of legality as possible."

George Washington explained why these lies work so well: ignorance provides the fertile soil for deception to grow.

"Ignorance & design, are difficult to combat. Out of these proceed illiberality, improper jealousies, and a train of evils which oftentimes, in republican governments, must be sorely felt before they can be removed. The former, that is ignorance, being a fit soil for the latter to work in."

GOOD NEWS

That's the bad news. The good news? Thomas Paine exposed the fatal weakness in their plan: they can never **force** anyone back to ignorance once they've broken through.

"Ignorance is of a peculiar nature: once dispelled, it is impossible to re-establish it. It is not originally a thing of itself, but is only the absence of knowledge; and though man may be kept ignorant, he cannot be made ignorant."

That means widespread ignorance is ultimately a choice. The solution, however, is no walk in the park.

Ignorance and obedience – those are easy. Knowledge and freedom? As Abigail Adams wrote, that takes relentless effort.

"Learning is not attained by chance; it must be sought for with ardor and attended to with diligence."

Getting the job done won't be quick and it won't be easy. We're all victims of a government-run "education" system. So there's no shame in starting from scratch.

The real disgrace, as Benjamin Franklin put it, is choosing to stay there.

"Being ignorant is not so much a Shame, as being unwilling to learn."

But that's not the end of the story. Ignorance alone is dangerous. As St. George Tucker pointed out, when combined with cowardice, it's fatal.

"When ignorance is united with supineness, liberty becomes lethargic, and despotism erects her standard without opposition."

With that one-two punch, liberty doesn't stand a chance.

BY CHOICE

"This can only end in despotism."

Benjamin Franklin didn't offer that as a theory. It was an indictment - and a prophetic one too. He knew exactly what happens when a people lack virtue: they tolerate or even beg for arbitrary power.

As a result, liberty dies and tyranny takes its place.

Not by accident. Not by force.

But by choice.

And he wasn't alone. The founders – and the political thinkers they learned from – understood this eternal truth: freedom cannot survive the corruption of the people. Not in a monarchy. Not in a republic. Not even in a system bound by the most carefully written constitution in human history.

Thomas Jefferson explained how it starts. The collapse of liberty doesn't begin with gunfire or invasions – it begins with an internal rot. A quiet, invisible corrosion that spreads through the people until the entire system breaks.

"It is the manners and spirit of the people which preserve a republic in vigor. A degeneracy in these is a canker which soon eats to the heart of its laws and constitution."

From there, the outcome is inevitable. The rules for government become meaningless. The tyrants rise. And the people, soft and submissive, cheer them on.

That's the path America has been on for years. Not because the country has been conquered. Because virtue decayed.

VIRTUE

Franklin was focused on character – because he knew freedom isn't granted, it's earned. And not everyone earns it.

"Only a virtuous people are capable of freedom. As nations become corrupt and vicious, they have more need of masters."

From there, James Madison dismissed the fantasy that liberty could be preserved by parchment alone.

If the people are corrupt, he warned, they won't just **tolerate** tyrants in office – they'll literally **vote** for them. And that makes every branch of government just as rotten as the people who put them there.

"To suppose that any form of government will secure liberty or happiness without any virtue in the people, is a chimerical idea. If there be sufficient virtue and intelligence in the community, it will be exercised in the selection of these men. So that we do not depend on their virtue, or put confidence in our rulers, but in the people who are to choose them."

DECAY

These weren't new insights. Algernon Sidney warned that liberty and virtue are inseparable.

"Liberty cannot be preserved, if the manners of the people are corrupted, nor absolute monarchy introduced where they are sincere."

He described parasites – people too corrupt, too soft, and too self-interested to even want to be free.

"Their slavish, vicious and base natures inclining them to seek only private and present advantages, they easily slide into a blind dependence upon one who has wealth and power."

Once that dependence takes root, nothing is too vile. They'll trade every principle they ever claimed to believe – for comfort.

"And desiring only to know his will, care not what injustice they do, if they may be rewarded. They worship what they find in the temple, tho it be the vilest of idols, and always like that best which is worst, because it agrees with their inclinations and principles."

Thomas Gordon, in his discourses on the Works of Tacitus, described the same decay in ancient Rome. But he wasn't just chronicling a famous political collapse – he was indicting a people so corrupted they had lost all capacity for freedom.

"They rendered the people idle, venal, vicious, insensible of private virtue, insensible of public glory or disgrace; but the things were liked, and the ends not seen, or not minded, so that they had their thorough effect."

The people weren't just passive – they accepted anything as long as they got their bread and circuses.

"And the Roman people, they who were wont to direct mighty wars, to raise and depose great Kings, to bestow or take away Empires, they who ruled the world, or directed its rule, were so sunk and debauched, that if they had but bread and shews, their ambition went no higher."

Even Machiavelli understood that tyranny doesn't just come from the top down. A corrupt people will stay enslaved no matter who is in charge - even if the tyrant is completely removed.

"It must be assumed as a well-demonstrated truth, that a corrupt people that lives under the government of a prince can never become free, even though the prince and his whole line should be extinguished."

In his discourses on the Roman historian Sallust, Gordon didn't blame the Republic's fall on the rulers. Analyzing the history, he placed the blame squarely on the people.

"Now such Fondness for Civil Disorders, and for the wicked Authors of such, is, by this Account, intirely derived from the depraved Spirit and Disposition of the People; and not imputable to the Misconduct of the Magistrates, however faulty they might be."

And he made it painfully clear: corrupt people won't just tolerate wicked rulers – they will hate the good, and worship the traitors.

"Nay, the best, the most strict and steady Administration must have been the most disliked and unpopular, when the People were passionate for the worst Calamities, such as Civil Dissentions and War; and for the wickedest Men, such as promoted those Calamities, and because they promoted them; even for Catiline, Cethegus, and every great Traitor and Incendiary."

SURRENDER

With a thorough knowledge of this history, John Dickinson saw how liberty really dies. It isn't taken at gunpoint. It's surrendered – willingly. Not because the people are incapable, but because they are either paralyzed by fear, or they have convinced themselves the government's abuses are perfectly legitimate.

"They voluntarily fasten their chains, by adopting a pusillanimous opinion, 'that there will be too much danger in attempting a remedy' – or another opinion no less fatal – 'that the government has a right to treat them as it does.'"

They make things worse when they rationalize and tell themselves that obedience is their duty. That submission is stability. And in doing so, they erase everything that made them free.

"They then seek a wretched relief for their minds, by persuading themselves, that to yield their obedience, is to discharge their duty. The deplorable poverty of spirit, that prostrates all the dignity bestowed by divine providence on our nature – of course succeeds."

Samuel Adams did not pull any punches. If the people lack the virtue needed to defend liberty, they earn contempt, not sympathy.

"If therefore a people will not be free; if they have not virtue enough to maintain their liberty against a presumptuous invader, they deserve no pity, and are to be treated with contempt and ignominy."

This standard grew out of knowledge - a deep understanding of the source of their rights - along with an unbreakable moral duty to do so, despite the odds stacked against them.

You can see the former reflected near the beginning of the Declaration of Independence.

"We hold these truths to be self-evident, that all men are created equal, that they are endowed by their Creator with certain unalienable Rights, that among these are Life, Liberty and the pursuit of Happiness."

While the latter is reflected in the solemn pledge at the end.

"And for the support of this Declaration, with a firm reliance on the protection of divine Providence, we mutually pledge to each other our Lives, our Fortunes and our sacred Honor."

That brings us back to Benjamin Franklin. On the final day of the Philadelphia Convention in 1787, he gave his approval to the newly drafted Constitution, but not without one final warning.

It likely raised some eyebrows then. It's prophetic now.

"This is likely to be well administered for a course of years, and can only end in Despotism, as other forms have done before it, when the people shall become so corrupted as to need despotic Government, being incapable of any other."

We were warned.

Not in secret. Not in vague terms. Openly. Repeatedly. By the people who knew firsthand how liberty is won – and how it's lost.

"We the People" didn't listen, but don't blame the tyrants. Blame the people who made them possible.

Chapter 13

HOW TO SPOT A REDCOAT

We are surrounded by redcoats.

They might not be part of King George's military, but their mindset is everywhere. It's not just in what they support, but also what they are willing to impose.

The founders and old revolutionaries didn't just fight an army. They fought a long, bloody war to secede from a system built on a set of views they considered a fate worse than death.

Here are the top-8 ways to spot a redcoat without ever seeing a uniform.

1. LOYALTY

The quickest way to spot a redcoat is one question: where does their loyalty lie?

Loyalty to a single person isn't patriotism. It's a complete rejection of the American Revolution. Decades before the War for Independence, Samuel Adams warned against allegiance to one individual.

"It is a very great Mistake to imagine that the Object of Loyalty is the Authority and Interest of one individual Man, however dignified by the Applause or enriched by the Success of Popular Actions."

Adams knew this as a student of history: loyalty to one man leads to tyranny and destruction.

"This has led Millions into such a degree of Dependance and Submission that they have at length found themselves oblig'd to homage the Instruments of their Ruin, at the very Time they were at Work to effect it."

John Adams saw the same kind of endgame for those who bend the knee to a political party, and flat-out refused to do it.

"I would quarrel with both parties, and with every individual of each, before I would subjugate my understanding, or prostitute my tongue or pen to either."

Some founders, like Noah Webster, saw party loyalty as the most dangerous of all.

"Nothing is more dangerous to the cause of truth and liberty than a party-spirit."

Loyalty to a person, a party, or even a nation? That's a redcoat. The American view? As Thomas Jefferson, John Dickinson, and the entire Second Continental Congress declared: loyalty belongs to liberty.

"Our attachment to no Nation upon earth should supplant our attachment to liberty."

2. RIGHTS

A redcoat believes rights are mere privileges.

Because they think the government - or even the Constitution itself - **grants** them their rights, they believe the government has the legitimate authority to regulate, restrict, license, or take them away.

In practice, they view liberty as a permission slip.

The American Revolution was built on the exact opposite. Rights are natural, unalienable, and pre-exist any government.

John Dickinson made it clear that true liberty does not come from politicians or pieces of paper.

"We claim them from a higher source - from the King of kings, and Lord of all the earth. They are not annexed to us by parchments and seals."

Alexander Hamilton agreed. He knew that if rights came from human documents, they could be erased by human hands.

"The sacred rights of mankind are not to be rummaged for, among old parchments, or musty records. They are written, as with a sun beam, in the whole volume of human nature, by the hand of the divinity itself; and can never be erased or obscured by mortal power."

People who think government gives you rights? They're redcoats.

The American view? Rights are not gifts from government. They don't come from documents - like a constitution or even a bill of rights. They are a gift from our Creator.

3. ARBITRARY POWER

But as Samuel Adams warned, liberty can't even exist where government does what it wants.

"It cannot indeed subsist in an arbitrary Government."

Whenever government action delivers what they want, a redcoat will gladly support it - constitutional limits be damned. The Americans had a specific term for that: arbitrary power. James Otis Jr. defined it this way:

"Arbitrary; which in plain English means no more than to do as one pleases."

A redcoat believes the government should be able to do as it pleases, as long as they agree with the policy or the outcome. It's even worse when that support is driven by blind loyalty to a specific politician or party. Either way, they make endless excuses for unconstitutional acts.

They will often claim it's no big deal - that it isn't affecting you, it doesn't cost much, or it's too small of a step to make a fuss about.

St. George Tucker warned that even the smallest step – the tiniest amount of arbitrary power – sets the precedent for even more in the future.

"Slight, and sometimes even imperceptible, innovations, occasional usurpations, founded upon the pretended emergency of the occasion: or upon former unconstitutional precedents."

They knew every single step beyond the limits of the Constitution is just a guarantee that the power will keep growing.. That's why George Washington called arbitrary power – usurpation – a **weapon** to destroy freedom.

"Let there be no change by usurpation; for though this, in one instance, may be the instrument of good, it is the customary weapon by which free governments are destroyed."

Despite these warnings, some will resort to the claim that "it's an emergency!" But as Samuel Adams put it, when people with power get to decide if they have extra power or funding for an "emergency," you'll end up with never-ending emergencies.

"Those Kings by the way, being the sole judges when emergencies happen, they generally create them as often as they want money."

The American view? James Otis Jr. summed it up best: arbitrary power is *"the curse and scandal of human nature,"* whatever the reason given for it.

4. WHO DECIDES

A redcoat believes the government gets to judge the limits of its own power.

When you point out an unconstitutional act, they might even agree, but only in theory. Ultimately, they take the position that it's not your call. It's up to the Supreme Court to decide. Or, if you can't convince the judges, you have to wait until you elect enough new politicians who not only agree with you, but are willing to repeal the act in question.

This is not a new idea. It is the exact mindset of the British empire.

In 1764, Royal Governor Sir Francis Bernard laid out the British view of sovereignty, declaring the government's power is *"absolute, uncontrollable, and accountable to none."*

People who believe the government gets the final say over its own limits hold the exact same view as the crown.

The founders understood the fatal flaw in this trap: if the government gets to decide what its limits are, it doesn't actually have any limits at all.

As Thomas Jefferson made clear in his Kentucky Resolutions of 1798, by taking this position, these redcoats put the opinions of the government about the Constitution above the Constitution itself.

"The Government created by this compact was not made the exclusive or final judge of the extent of the powers delegated to itself; since that would have made its discretion, and not the constitution, the measure of its powers."

John Dickinson made the same case at the height of the Revolution. Government is the hired help. So the people themselves get to decide when government goes too far.

"They will always have the same rights, that all free states have, of judging when their privileges are invaded, and of using all prudent measures for preserving them."

Those who believe the government gets to dictate the extent of its own power? They're redcoats.

The American view? The government is not at the top of the food chain. The people have the final say.

5. OBEDIENCE

The next - and one of the most obvious ways - to spot a redcoat is that they demand obedience. The people have no right to decide that government acts are beyond the limits of the constitution - and by logical extension, they have no right to do anything other than obey what government tells them to obey.

Patrick Henry helped amplify the American view - when government goes beyond its limits, the people *"are not bound to yield obedience."*

Going beyond just moral and legal requirements, John Dickinson brought it forward into the realm of strategy too. Compliance with arbitrary power, he wrote, is a test of the backbone of the people because it sets the precedent for total tyranny.

"If you quietly bend your Necks to that Yoke, you prove yourselves

ready to receive any Bondage to which your Lords and Masters shall please to subject you."

Putting these principles together, no one summed up the American view better than James Otis, Jr.

"He that would palm the doctrine of unlimited passive obedience and non-resistance upon mankind, is not only a fool and a knave, but a rebel against common sense, as well as the laws of God, of Nature, and his Country."

6. STANDING ARMIES

That brings us to the next way to spot a redcoat, and their favorite: standing armies. When they use arbitrary power, they need the muscle to enforce it, especially if the people decide to refuse to comply.

They are always sold as a tool of safety, but as John Dickinson warned, they are in fact the *"engine of arbitrary power."* And that engine, as Joseph Warren made clear, will *"always endanger the liberty"* of the people.

Not sometimes. Not most of the time.

Always.

Gen. Henry Knox explained that this danger is greatest in times of peace.

"Whatever may be the efficacy of a standing army in war, it cannot in peace be considered as friendly to the rights of human nature."

George Mason also warned there is no special exemption for America: a standing army is a threat to liberty anywhere and everywhere it exists.

"When once a standing army is established in any country, the people lose their liberty."

Because of this understanding, there was little that drew the ire of the founders and old revolutionaries more than standing armies.

In the American view, they were considered, as Jonathan Mason put it, the *"scourge of the innocent."*

7. DUTY

A redcoat thinks defending liberty is reckless.

When the people refuse to comply and government sends in the muscle to force the issue, a redcoat always points the blame in the same direction - not at the tyrant wielding arbitrary power, but the people who dare to defy it.

To a redcoat, the troublemaker is always the one who won't bow. Order - any order, at any price - is the highest virtue. And the ones who take more active measures in response? Their resistance is "extremism."

Samuel Adams left no room for doubt. Defending the constitution and liberty isn't an option, it's duty.

"It is our duty to defend them against all attacks."

How they meet that duty depends on the threat. A free people reach for the most peaceful means first, exactly as Simeon Howard described.

"Reason with, and persuade the adversary to desist, if there be opportunity for it; or get out of his way, if he can; and if by such means he can prevent the injury, he is to use no other."

The redcoat knows this moral approach well - and they work to exploit it. So they counsel patience. Endlessly. It is never the right time to take more active measures in response. The danger is always too great, the cost always too high. And anyone who says otherwise is a dangerous radical.

But when a tyrant persists - and the worst of them always do - those methods run out. Joseph Hawley knew: patience that never ends isn't patience. It's surrender.

"The people or state who will not or cannot defend their liberties and rights will not have any for any long time."

The Declaration of Independence answered the redcoat view head on. When arbitrary power becomes the design, resistance is not just a good idea, it's a moral requirement.

"When a long train of abuses and usurpations, pursuing invariably the same Object evinces a design to reduce them under absolute Despotism, it is their right, it is their duty, to throw off such Government, and to provide new Guards for their future security."

8. IGNORANCE AND VICE

A redcoat wants you dumb and corrupt.

Spotting the first seven takes effort. You have to know the Constitution, study the history, and reason through the principles.

A redcoat would rather you be told what to think by the government, its "education" system, or their favorite party. They prefer a credentialed class anointed to do the thinking for everyone. Just trust the experts.

Samuel Adams named the formula: that is exactly how tyranny survives and thrives.

"It is in the Interest of Tyrants to reduce the People to Ignorance and Vice."

Thomas Paine knew why. Ignorance obeys.

"Reason obeys itself; and Ignorance submits to whatever is dictated to it."

And Thomas Jefferson couldn't have been more clear: ignorance and freedom will never coexist.

"If a nation expects to be ignorant and free ... it expects what never was and never will be."

But ignorance is only half of it. The other half is vice. A people too soft, too comfortable, and too self-interested to defend their own liberty will trade it away for ease - and a redcoat will lead the charge.

Samuel Adams found that mentality absolutely repugnant.

"If therefore a people will not be free; if they have not virtue enough to maintain their liberty against a presumptuous invader, they deserve no pity, and are to be treated with contempt and ignominy."

That is the one-two punch. An ignorant people can't recognize the redcoats. A corrupt people will not even bother. Together, as St. George Tucker warned, liberty doesn't stand a chance.

"When ignorance is united with supineness, liberty becomes lethargic, and despotism erects her standard without opposition."

Those who would rather outsource thinking and surrender virtue for comfort? That's a redcoat.

The American view? Freedom is earned - with knowledge, virtue, and the courage to use both.

Made in the USA
Coppell, TX
25 June 2026

83473246R00071